BITE YOUR BULLET
CALL THE SHOTS

VIJAY LUHAR

authorHOUSE

AuthorHouse™ UK
1663 Liberty Drive
Bloomington, IN 47403 USA
www.authorhouse.co.uk
Phone: UK TFN: 0800 0148641 (Toll Free inside the UK)
UK Local: 02036 956322 (+44 20 3695 6322 from outside the UK)

© 2021 Vijay Luhar. All rights reserved.

No part of this book may be reproduced, stored in a retrieval system, or transmitted by any means without the written permission of the author.

Published by AuthorHouse 08/16/2021

ISBN: 978-1-6655-8546-0 (sc)
ISBN: 978-1-6655-8547-7 (hc)
ISBN: 978-1-6655-8548-4 (e)

Print information available on the last page.

Any people depicted in stock imagery provided by Getty Images are models, and such images are being used for illustrative purposes only.
Certain stock imagery © Getty Images.

This book is printed on acid-free paper.

Because of the dynamic nature of the Internet, any web addresses or links contained in this book may have changed since publication and may no longer be valid. The views expressed in this work are solely those of the author and do not necessarily reflect the views of the publisher, and the publisher hereby disclaims any responsibility for them.

CONTENTS

A Word from the Author vii
Preface ix
Introduction xiii

Chapter 1   Where Are You Now, and Do You Know Yourself? 1
Chapter 2   The Oxymoron of the Comforting Bullet 17
Chapter 3   What Goals Do You Have? 23
Chapter 4   Confidence-Building 34
Chapter 5   Shining Your Light in Your Personal Life 47
Chapter 6   Boundary-Setting 59
Chapter 7   Assured Body Language and More
            Confidence-Builders 72
Chapter 8   Relationships 84
Chapter 9   Your Relationship with Time 97
Chapter 10 Energy Management 106
Chapter 11 Leading 114
Chapter 12 Mental Fitness: Recharging Oneself 138
Chapter 13 Physical Fitness: Bulletproofing Mind and Body 148
Chapter 14 Icing on the Cake: The Winning Mentality 159
Chapter 15 Conclusion: Aligning the Choices We Make with
            Our Ultimate Desire 170

A WORD FROM THE AUTHOR

Having just completed the writing of *Bite Your Bullet*, I am certain this is a success. A win. The emotion I felt when writing the last lines of the last chapter confirm to me that we are all powerful.

The goal of *Bite Your Bullet* is for us all to really value who we are. I often see people talking the talk without taking action. I never knew it happened so much. People tell themselves things like *I can't* or *I am not confident enough*, confirming the lack in their own lives and abilities. I was really frustrated and annoyed that people were not utilising their own power they had within.—the potential I see in everyone. I promise I can identify a quality that every person possesses which is most likely a gift they are afraid to express.

I have seen empathetic people get walked over by others because they are putting others first all the time and being taken advantage of. *Bite Your Bullet* tells of a truthful journey that will leave you feeling bulletproof. It is a journey that never stops. I will give you the key to unlock your inner power and destroy any negative perceptions you have of yourself. The time for everyone to bite their bullet is here, as the world is relying on us to become more independent and not rely on authority figures. We are the ones in control of our lives.

Being in the hands of the authorities or government is no way to lead a fulfilling life. I am not speaking of a rebellion against higher powers. I am suggesting that we take our own minds and make them bulletproof against the rat race habits created by the years of repetitive conditioning that have taken place in the modern world. Previous generations have been conditioned not to think for themselves, and this has been passed on to us. No matter what generation you are from and what you have been through, the power in the chapters ahead will ignite your inner being to love life fully or fall in love with life again.

If you are a nerd, be proud of being a nerd. A sporty person, be proud of that. A loud person, own it, be proud. A quiet person, own that too, and be proud. Besides being quiet, loud, sporty, or nerdy, make sure you are happy! If you are quiet and you wish you were more assertive, then you will be unlocked as you read ahead. If you are nerdy and feel separate from others at times, you will find your answers here to express yourself and feel strong for being yourself. Are you a sporty person and not confident in other areas? This will encourage you to transfer your qualities elsewhere. If you have been through any traumas, the fact that you are taking steps and discovering a different element of yourself shows how strong and powerful you are not let your history dictate the way you live at present.

Bite Your Bullet is a journey to becoming bulletproof and ever ready—mentally, emotionally, and physically. Be patient and understanding with yourself, as your journey to bulletproof power could require continuous reminders of the techniques given. For now, it's one step at a time. I wish you the best ahead—now, always, and forever.

PREFACE

Bite your bullet. What does that mean to you? Think about it for a moment. Write it down and brainstorm what you believe this might mean.

Bite the bullet is a common phrase that has been used for many years. It suggests an unpleasant situation which is unavoidable, and you must bite the bullet to get through it and face the consequences. That to me is living in hope and not being in full control of your environment. *Bite your bullet* has a very different meaning. It describes our power and right to navigate our lives with authenticity and trust in the future outcome of our actions.

Where do you want to be in life? What is happening in your life right now that you don't like? What opportunities are you afraid of taking? How are you going to achieve your goals? Where are you going to start your goals? *How, when, if, what, but, because*—all of these questions and words are there for what? How is your goal hindered by all these expressions, and more importantly, who created them?

In *Bite Your Bullet*, you'll learn how our limiting beliefs have created invisible barriers. As you read on, it is highly important to take action. There are action steps for when you are in your own space to really have your pen and paper or word processor open for completing the tasks. No one in the world can help us more than ourselves. The action steps you will see throughout *Bite Your Bullet* are there to be completed so you can evaluate your current state of mind and how to progress in all areas of your life.

I suggest you have a folder set up and file all your learnings away to look back on in the later chapters and for whenever you need or want to view them. This can be an investment and not just a fun, temporary read. If you are reading this on your train commute or a place where you are unable to write, or if you feel comfortable starting the writing later after you've read through it first, then by all means take that route instead. The commitment aspect to me is extremely important and the only way the material in this book will be of any benefit to anyone. It is all in your hands.

What Is *Bite Your Bullet*?

The bullet is a metaphor for the blocks you create in your mind. How many times have you wanted to do something but were held back by a fear within you that stopped you from taking that step? Starting a fitness regime, starting your own business, striking up a conversation with a stranger, enrolling in a new course—these are just a few moments I have highlighted, and there are many more where we have created a mental bullet in front of us.

Imagine yourself sitting on a chair in a room with a desk, a piece of paper, and a pen on the table. You can focus on any goal you like. You have written down your goals and are excited about where this can take you and how important it is to progress in your own life.

Now imagine you are holding a piece of paper in your hands with your goal written on it. As you sit there in this empty room with your desk, chair, pen, and paper, fear overtakes you. You start to believe you cannot achieve your goals.

Finally, imagine a bullet in front of you, spinning in the air, not moving close to your forehead but not moving away from you. The gun of fear has been fired, and the bullet is teasing you by appearing to not penetrate your brain. Unknown to you, however, it already has.

The bullet represents your fears and insecurities. This bullet could have been created by a family member, friend, or someone you have seen on social media or TV. You have no trust in yourself, and you block your success by creating an imaginary bullet in front of you, ready to kill your dreams.

What has compelled me to write this book is the fact that people have taken away their own power by creating their own bullet to overshadow their true potential. Lack of expression and self-belief creates these imaginary bullets of fear to hinder our destiny or our true potential. You are extremely talented, and others around you have talents too. How many bullets are people facing on a daily basis?

Throughout our journey through the chapters ahead, there are examples I have referenced from my own life. The purpose of these examples is to highlight that the impossible is possible. My goal is to inspire others and not by any means to blow my own trumpet and shout about my successes to make myself feel good. If I did this on a regular basis just to elevate my ego, I would be living in fear and having to grab on to the previous successes I had. But I know I shall continue achieving for the rest of my life.

Speaking about yourself positively and proudly should be encouraged to align your actions with your words. My request is for you all to draw from my experiences and look at the deeper message behind each example and how you can apply it to your personality.

What Form Does the Bullet Come In?

We often imagine the worst-case scenarios of what could go wrong and how it could go wrong. Why do we have this feeling? We do not need to feel robbed of our desires to succeed in life or succeed at anything.

A simple example is the choice to eat healthy food as opposed to junk food. In simple terms, buying fruit and veg, stocking up your fridge with these items, and throwing away the junk food is easy. The bullet comes in the form of excuses of why you cannot do this.

The key word in the phrase *Bite your bullet* is *your*. You have the power. You are the one creating your bullet. You are the one who is able to bite your bullet. Biting your fears and insecurities away empowers you to take control of your life and destroy that bullet. The explosion of breaking through your fears and insecurities reminds you of who you are and what your true self is.

Life is win-win. Your actions benefit yourself and inspire those around you. Move forward with me in discovering your power to bite your bullet before it kills your mind's eye, your vision of how you want to live your life. What happens when you bite your bullet? Simple: you crush the imaginary enemy within holding you back. The firepower within the bullet is transmuted as energy for you to move forward with what you want to become. That is the power of *Bite Your Bullet*.

INTRODUCTION

The following is stated with no ego. It is stated assure all readers that anyone can feel this way. I believe in myself, and you can believe in yourself too.

People from various walks of life often wonder, *How can I be a strong leader?* and *How can I can lead a team?* If many people have been feeling this, there must be something meaningful about it. I recently had a globally renowned energy practitioner say to me, "Don't underestimate your power as a life coach. You have a lot to give." The room was filled with people, and he singled me out. I felt a wave of energy take me over at that point. It was time to really go deep into myself and find out what is my purpose with my gift.

For many of us, the idea of winning surrounds us, engrosses us, becomes us. For others, the comfort of not winning is their journey—one to be respected. Everyone's time for winning comes at one point or another. Winning has no single definition, as small victories are victories nonetheless.

When children receive a toy they have spent weeks and months pestering their parents for, that is their victory. Students making it through all their exams with a passing grade is a win for them to get into college or university. Some students may class achieving good or excellent grades a win. They are all winners in their own way, as they got what they wanted. However, the winning mentality end goal I am talking about is the students who challenged themselves to achieve all A grades.

Every one of us is capable of achieving the biggest win we can think of. Clichés about believing in yourself are true. Believing in yourself evolves into knowing yourself. This is the first step to gaining the power of winning that we all desire.

For the leader, the belief you put into your teams will increase, creating a chain of winning power. You will get your team members to believe and recognise their abilities and at the same time increase in confidence. You'll create a team of individual winners and finally a winning team.

My Own Journey in a Nutshell

My own story is a journey of sixteen years of discovering my talents of self-belief, which led me to know myself. *Bite Your Bullet* can keep you from having to go through the same sixteen-year journey. I have taken my gift of "the best" mentality to share with the world.

As a child, I always use to find myself saying "the best." I don't know why I used to say this, but I just used to like being the best and saying "the best." In my early childhood years, the best to me was in sports—karate and video games. I was very good at these, as I had that focus and respect for those areas.

One thing I lacked back then was the decisive killer instinct for karate. I was very good, but I was not confident enough to win in sparring competitions, as I was afraid to express myself. Expressing myself in front of my friends was fine; expressing myself in front of strangers, I was not confident enough to do at the time.

During a karate competition I punched an opponent in the face and heard a number of gasps from the audience. I was told to calm it down by the referee. I then eased off on my opponent, with less power in my strikes, and I lost the contest on points. I look back on that moment as funny; I easily could have won, but I was not applying myself passionately enough.

This came down to not expressing myself in all walks of life. The expressive self is highly important to show the world who you are and what you are made of. By not expressing myself and going into my shell, so to speak, after the referee told me to calm the strikes down, I became less interested in winning than in pleasing the referee.

I then became very well known for my talent at football. I was free-flowing and playing the game passionately. This was the foundation for my confidence to grow, as I got a lot of attention from this from the older children in the years above me. I then began a rebellious streak in school, and I was able to express myself, as opposed to the karate days of being reserved. The lesson in rebelliousness was to transmute that energy into achieving. I'll expand on this later.

This "best" attitude did branch out into my interests in high school, which were physical education, sports, drama, and getting a girlfriend. Yes, these were my priorities at the time. The girlfriend one was a priority, funny enough, but at that time that was part of my win.

I was a stubborn teenager and did not have a care for education like maths, English, and science. I did well in English, as I enjoyed the creative aspect of this, but school subjects in general were more to do with what I found interesting as opposed to aiming to achieve good grades. I encourage everyone to really achieve with your grades in school, college, uni, etc., as it is an expression/extension of yourself. Consider your grades extra tools to have in your locker.

The college years brought more socially based goals, and I did not have a care for grades until it came to the subject of drama and theatre studies, which I did very well in, even landing an audition at a top international drama school. It was only when I got to university that I began to take education seriously, with a foundation year. Something switched within me, as years of paying no attention to school subjects caught up with me. University was all about setting myself up for the future.

Fees were involved this time too, and my parents were not happy with my performance and my grades. It was all or nothing at this point. The one university that accepted me on this foundation course was a platform to the three-year full degree after that. This was my moment to become interested in academic modules.

The focus and determination that grew in me was evident. I was head and shoulders above the rest of the students, who were from a wide variety of backgrounds and ages. I was even approached by students who were older than me to become the head of the class, which involves putting yourself forward to attend meetings with the campus authorities. I did not join this, but I was honoured to be considered.

I gained a distinction grade in my first year, and my retake for GCSE maths achieved an A grade. In my first round of GCSE in high school, I'd achieved a D grade, which was a fail. My focus was split between being a weekend manager for a department store and university.

A lot of people suggest doing something you enjoy, and this was what happened with me. On the weekends, I would lead a whole store on the front line of customer service, and I felt like a real leader. I *was* a real leader! The weekend managers before me I felt could have connected better with the team in a more rapport-building way, as no one was given any direction. When I took over the role, I connected with my team with a passion to win our targets.

I always saw myself as a warrior and someone who is fearless, whether it be speaking to upper management or decision-making in general. This self-belief bounced back between my weekend job and my university work. I was always first to be the leader in group work and always willing to push myself to make my group the best—not in a way where it was just dependant on me as the one taking all the glory but encouraging my peers to share their ideas. That focus in an academic environment had never been self-encouraged by me up until this point. That first success back in football times in school is where the journey was unlocked for me, and it branched out into a sense of pride in every other area of my life ever since then.

I put myself forward in becoming a branch manager. I led successful teams every step of the way in each store I managed. The results I achieved were sometimes considered unachievable with regards to the targets each store gets measured on. This has given me the confidence in projecting my no-fear attitude to be able to take on any challenge set for me. I know I can achieve. My teams have been encouraged by me to achieve, and I have unlocked their potential.

Often, I explain to the students who work part-time for me how they can use the job as a platform for their future. They can describe how they were part of a winning team and what their input was.

This has been my proudest accomplishment. I have created win-win situations for me and my team; they have assisted me in achieving a desired result to be the best, and they have in turn increased their ability to meet their future with confidence.

The Root

As you read on, we'll go into the root of our human journey. I have stated in job interviews that I look at the root causes of everything in the stores and teams I manage, whether operations in the store and layouts of working to the health and safety or people issues taking place. It is no coincidence that I have done this in every store I have managed, and with every store team, we managed to have the best performing teams.

The root cause for me remains our approach to a situation. I have been doing this all my life, and you would notice it too. How we do anything is how we do everything—a phrase coined by the spiritual practitioner mentioned earlier. This phrase is something I have always done throughout my whole life, and when I connect the dots of my history, it makes sense that I have come to this particular outcome in my life.

How I did anything was how I did everything. Whether it was playing football or working as a sales advisor in a department store or working out in the gym—my intensity was the same everywhere. This root of a person is the root of all things.

That is why, when I started managing any store team, I would meet each of the team members individually and discuss what they were about. I would take time to get to know their ambitions and how these fit with the overall goal. Some were disengaged, and I knew I had to monitor them and coach them to achieve. For those who were excelling and looking for growth, I was able to provide that for them. I promoted many people and continued to follow my win-win mentality.

The root of all our success or failure is the imaginary bullet we create. This determines how we approach a situation. For example, when we are at work, we can be thoroughly organised and clinical. Yet when we get home, we can be the total opposite and be disorganised and messy. There is no right or wrong here. The answer to personal growth is already there. If we are organised at work but not at home, it is possible to approach the home situation in the same manner and see how you feel at home and how content you feel with approaching all areas of your life that way.

You know where your keys at home are, as you have a set place for them. You know where you placed your paperwork, as you organised your folder of house bills. You know what you have placed in your garage for what you need when you want to wash the car or find certain tools you need to finish off a task. This organised energy you create will remind you what you are capable of doing, as you have structured yourself.

This can also be a signal of how not to approach a situation. If you are in social settings/romantic settings, you don't want to be structured to a tee, like you are at work. You have to not expect an outcome and enjoy the moment. Those who are in your presence will be there when you are authentic, without expectations. The lesson is always in the root cause of everything.

When you internalise the *bite your bullet* mentality, you will understand the deepness of the root we cover as we go forward. It will challenge you to look at uncomfortable situations and may remind you of who you are and bring up feelings you have avoided for so long. Bite your bullet, and don't be afraid of learning who you are. You will thank yourself for it in the long run.

Everyone Can Benefit

As I write this down, I feel a sense of pride filling me. It is motivating me to push forward in life and achieve even more. This is the spark and passion I want you all to feel as you read these words. You and I are on the same team now: the winning team. My energy going into this book with my words flowing through me onto this keyboard is the passion and intensity I feel when gearing up my teams and really achieving a goal. In fact, make that many goals.

Everything mentioned above will be expanded upon throughout our journey of *Bite Your Bullet*. The determination you have shown to be the best leader you can be is the greatest gift you can give to yourself. You are biting your bullet, and I give thanks that I am able to assist you in your journey to succeeding and bringing up all areas of your life. When I say *leading*, I mean bringing out the leader in yourself.

The outlook in *Bite Your Bullet* is useful to beginners who are finding out who they are. It doesn't matter if you are 15 years old or 70; you can be a beginner at any age. Parents can benefit from this by assisting their child's development of confidence and self-love, which is not taught in schools. The generation coming up today are the brightest individuals out there and are very sharp. They are more highly aware of their surroundings and how our actions have an impact on the environment and the planet as a whole. The next generations are already brave enough to express themselves on social media and be their own leaders. With the right guidance, these are the leaders of a positive, progressive tomorrow.

Bite Your Bullet will resonate with people who are living life through their sensory experiences and are happy with this. When I say *sensory experience*, I mean the physical world around us and the enjoyment of socialising, partying, fitness goals, etc. I still enjoy parties and materialistic behaviours, as life is there to enjoy.

Bite Your Bullet will also resonate with people who are living a spiritual journey. I have been going through this for many years now but have ignored it until very recently. The metaphysical level of spirituality means utilising this power in our everyday lives to connect mind, body, and soul. It will resonate with you when you experience those levels at some point in your life. The darkest hours in your life are where you will discover the strength within to grow.

Stages of life have no right or wrong. They are just where you are. Some people are happy to stay in their zone for a longer period of time as opposed to consciously making that decision of where they want to be. As life evolves in front of us, all the tools I want to share with you will lead you through any stage. You will be able to navigate out of the lowest of lows and soar higher in the highest of highs. This understanding I share is more powerful than just your career goals. It involves your quality of living as a human being and awareness of yourself that will improve and allow you to recognise the potential in yourself and in others.

Applying a Bulletproof Mindset

The following highlights of my career are shared to demonstrate how I was working with self-belief from the age of 17. You can become aware of other people's potential through their actions and assist them in developing their winning mentality.

I mentioned that in university, I was working part-time as a weekend manager in a department store. Prior to that, my part-time job was as a sales advisor. I got the job at the time thanks to my sister, who was in management in that store. It was my first time earning my own money. I stayed there for around two years, starting at the age of 17.

I remember the day I handed in my notice. I'd found out that two colleagues had been promoted to the position of weekend manager. At that time, I was living with my family and the majority of my expenses were paid by my parents. I decided to leave out of pride and ego. Looking back on it, there are pros and cons to that choice, One thing I am proud of is that I walked away from a situation where I felt I was not growing.

When it came to my university years, I checked with my old employer to see if there was a weekend manager role available. I was informed by two of the staff that the current weekend managers were leaving. Long story short, I was rehired.

I made it very clear in the interview that I want to be a weekend manager. I had that firm fixation that I could lead the team on the weekends whilst studying at university. They started me off as a customer service desk advisor, which was a step up from sales advisor and was a requirement in order to make it to weekend manager level. There I learnt certain aspects of the job I did not see before.

At this point, I was behaving and acting like a senior member of the team. Often, a lot of the team would ask me questions, as they looked up to me. That feeling I had within me that I would lead was projected in my aura to my colleagues. They trusted me regarding certain complex matters.

After around three months, the conversation finally came up regarding the weekend manager position. The assistant manager at the time was speaking to me regarding the role. He stated that the previous weekend managers were not performing to the required standard, which did not surprise me. I knew that a yes-man had been promoted. I was far from a yes-man myself. I always respected the hierarchy. but I would never lose my sense of identity or have my views brushed under the carpet.

The way the job was sold to me was that my pay would stay the same but my hours would increase. The assistant manager at the time thought he was being clever saying this to a 20-year-old, but I was well aware of how this was working. Yet it wasn't my concern. My concern was getting into the job role and progression opportunity.

I became fully immersed in the role, managing all types of situations, whether with customers, staff, or operations. At this point in my part-time role, my main objective was always the customer service element. I was proud of this leadership role. I found myself getting the highest marks in my class for my university modules, as I was just flowing with enthusiasm. Playing indoor football with new friends in university helped me make connections. I was good at football, and I believe this helped me on a social level.

Continuing My Career

After university, my main goal was to get into work as quickly as possible. My cousin was getting married the year I graduated, and we had planned a family trip to India for his wedding. All of us cousins, aunts, uncles, etc. travelled from London to India. It was great fun and the best thing ever to spend three weeks abroad in a different environment with relatives you see in London.

I thoroughly enjoyed myself, but I was itching to get back to London to start my career. When I returned, I had an email from an assessment centre for graduates. Overeager, I called them straight away and only had three days to prepare when usually it was two weeks on average. I had to come up with a presentation talking about anything for three minutes. There were group exercises, and we were constantly analysed by the assessment teams.

I thought I had done enough, as I did take the lead in the group situations. However, I did not make it through to that day. My three-minute presentation wasn't given the full preparation it deserved, and that is where I missed out.

There was a competing assessment centre, and I decided to prepare better for this one. I had one week this time. Long story short, I made it through as a very strong candidate. This statement was made by the assessment centre staff. They were very impressed with me. A combination of determination, resilience, and preparation played a vital role in my success.

This company found me a job in sales with a small IT firm in North London. This was an office-based role. I kept my job as weekend manager at the department store, so I was working seven days straight at this point, but I was fine. The office-based role was something new for me, as I had no freedom to roam a large store and be on my toes constantly. It was quite mundane, and I wasn't enjoying it at all. I felt like I had lost all my leadership qualities and was becoming a robot. I picked up the phone and made cold calls to IT firms. It's a business strategy that works, of course. However, it was not for me.

The final push for me to get out of there was my boss at the time throwing tantrums at everyone on a daily basis. Just to paint a picture for you: he was a small man, about five foot two in height, and he would shout at the top of his lungs to be heard. If you were not picking up the phone and you were typing something on the computer, he would slam the table with his hands and shout at the team and swear, "Fucking come on! You're a sales team. You get paid to pick up the phone." There were a few other new starters with me at the time, and this approach did not sit well with any of us. The on-edge feeling was always there.

Despite all this, I planned to implement the positive mindset I had set myself. I made some good connections with a few top law firms for their IT equipment. Regardless of the situation around me, I was focussing on the job at hand.

It did not sit well with my boss that I did not attend the Christmas party they decided to throw for the team. I wasn't really into socialising with the boss at the time or being fake. This is a good reminder for us all to take away about being true to ourselves.

When the weekend came, I was back at the department store managing the team. Even though this was work, it felt like I was in my natural element again, taking the lead and impacting the store's targets. Yet I handed in my resignation with two months' notice in order to focus on the full-time office job. In the long run, working seven days continuously would have burnt me out.

At the IT sales job, we all pitched in to keep the office clean. We would all rotate with the washing up or making tea. One Friday in the office, my boss shouted at me, as I was washing the dishes with "cold water" (his words). He shouted, "Why the fuck are you washing the dishes like this? Fucking hell, Vijay …"

In that moment, I had two ways to bite my bullet. I could have thrown the plate at him or against the wall. Instead, I remained cool and let him continue in front of the whole team. I stayed quiet and calm, and it was the correct decision. He then came up to me later and said, "It's good you're washing the dishes."

I am proud of the way I conducted myself at the time, as I did not lose my cool. I had that temper at times growing up in my teens, but I had learned a lot with regards to positivity in the few years before that incident, and this allowed me to handle that particular situation with silence and dignity.

I was 23 at this point, and the staff could see the boss's behaviour and how inappropriate it was. He had done this to everyone in terms of the shouting at the top of his voice and attempting to intimidate his team. I walked away from the building that night on the Friday and decided I didn't need to be there any longer.

I went into the department store on the weekend and asked the store manager if I could retract my resignation. Thank the stars above, the lady she had hired to replace me had to pull out of the role, and it was an easy transition for me to continue. However, this time I stated I want to go full-time, not just weekends anymore. I had decided I wanted to become a branch manager.

It was all set. My career path for progression was in front of me. I was not looking sideways or backwards. The push away from an office job given to me by that boss was my angel leading me onto my path. I was at my happiest leading a team and impacting results, not being a robot sitting at a desk all day.

This was the start of my journey of achieving my goal of becoming a branch manager, and I was ready to go at 100 miles per hour. The fixed goal cleared any bullets from my mind. I had laid out the career path in front of me, and more importantly, I was approaching it with a clear mind and pure heart.

I have always stated that an honest victory without putting others down is the truest path to take in achieving your goals. This is what creates fearlessness within you. No matter if anyone attempts to put you down or discourages you from a goal, you know you are a fearless warrior in your power to succeed.

Bite Your Bullet does not limit you to your career goals. *Bite Your Bullet* will show you how to apply everything to all areas of your life. I will return to the story above of how I bit my bullets and led winning teams in every store I managed. For now, it is time to focus on you and any potential bullets arising in your mind's eye.

CHAPTER 1

Where Are You Now, and Do You Know Yourself?

To the high school/college student: Are you coasting through your modules and enjoying the social life? Or are you academically focussed on your grades and have no social life?

To the university student: Have you completed your course and are now deciding on a career path? Or are you midway through your course and have messed up your grades by partying too much?

To working people in non-office jobs: Are you progressing in your job role? Do you want to progress in your job role? Do you hate your job? Do you love your job?

To office workers: Are you working twelve-hour days like a slave to the system? Are you taking care of your health and putting yourself first? Are you doing drugs to escape the intensity of work pressures? Are you being fake to yourself and others? Are you progressing to where you want to be?

To service men and women—nurses, police, paramedics, military: Are you in it for your country? Are you in it for the people? Are you extremely stressed in what you do? Have you reached out for help for your mental state of mind? Are you corrupt? Can we trust you? The whole country looks up to you.

To actors/footballers/celebrities: Are you living the dream? Is your personal life healthy? When was the last time you connected with friends and family? What is your message to all your followers? Have drugs helped you (if you have taken any, that is)?

To pensioners/elderly: What goals do you wish you could have achieved? What goals do you want to achieve? Are you finally putting yourself first? Are you taking care of your health? Do you miss the fire in your belly? How are you going to get it back? Are you scared of dying with regrets?

To parents: Are you unlocking your child's potential? What is the bullet you are holding in front of yourself with regards to being the best parent you can be? What legacy do you want to leave your children? How do you know your children are in their own power?

All of the above are places people want to be at or are striving to get to. Anyone can be in any of these places, and we are all looking to fall into the elderly category at some point in our lives; ageing is inevitable. Where are you now? The questions above are the most common questions we see posed to those in that particular environment. I am not a socialite where I have met a number of celebrities, but judging by the interviews and highs and lows we see them share with us, these are the questions posed to them. The point is that all of us have a bullet holding us prisoner to our own confinement.

By recognising where you are now, you are beginning to know yourself. It is too easy to forget who you are. When my friends and I were in university, we felt like we had an unlimited amount of time to enjoy the world. We laughed more often than not. We were in a place of freedom. By *freedom*, I mean socially, we could interact with whoever we wanted to. We had the freedom to do our work or not, the freedom to choose when we want to socialise with our close friends. At that time, we did not realise that we were just experiencing the moment.

My friends and I have been discussing this recently—how the working life takes over and you become so accustomed to the intense grind that you forget who you are. The decision-making for your personal life seems constrained by time, as we are on the clock of the company we work for. If you are running your own business, you are on the clock of your own deadlines. These moments where we don't put ourselves first anymore is where we can lose ourselves.

Don't get me wrong, high school/college/uni students—you can also get into this losing-yourself category. For example, you can lose yourself in a romantic relationship. If everything is rosy between you and your lover, you are losing your former self, or maybe you've given up things you once did with your friends. The other side is going through a break-up with a romantic partner. These moments of emotional trauma can really break you—but break you to grow. It's at this moment you do not know who you are anymore. If you're partying hard with your uni friends and have neglected your education, you may wonder who you have become, lost in procrastination. All these moments remind you of what you have lost, and the person you have lost is yourself.

Emotional traumas are not limited to student life. They can happen to anyone and at any time. How prepared are you for those moments? Some of us have trained our minds through positive conditioning, building the resilience within ourselves to handle any situation. Remember, these moments of pain are there to rebuild us, and there is no other solution but to experience that pain. Depressed feelings are there to be experienced. They are the worst feelings at the time, but the worst thing to do is turn to antidepressants, drugs, or alcohol, where you mask the pain.

All of these losing-yourself moments are bullets we begin to create. They are right in front of us for days, weeks, months, and in many cases years, as we have not bitten our own bullet and confronted the trauma head-on. The bullet is in front of us, swirling by our head. If you have gone through an emotional trauma of loss, you have to experience that emotion of the lowest of lows. By going through the process, you find out who you can become. You have to bite your bullet in these cases. It is when you have destroyed your bullet that your mind will begin the healing process and the stages of rebuilding. I promise you that you will be a new person and feel evolved.

Going out to a party when you have an assignment due is a bullet you have created for yourself. You are avoiding the important issue of completing your goal of an assignment. Workers who struggle with money, failing to budget and spending lavishly, are creating their bullet by wasting their earned money on material items to boost their own ego. These are bullets, again, you are creating for yourself. Believing that you cannot save money and spending it on instant gratification such as alcohol (I mean excessive consumption) is diverting you from your true power.

Believing that you can achieve what you want to achieve is the first step to knowing yourself. The action steps you will take to support your belief system will create the confidence to realise who you are.

Office workers who get caught in what is commonly known as the rat race and forget who they are have a greater risk of declining health, both physically and mentally. Why have you accepted this bullet you created? It is spinning in front of you, following you everywhere you go, not giving you a minute to yourself. It is time to reclaim your power and be who you want to be.

There are some office workers who have come out of the corporate environment to start up their own business. They took their power back and followed their passion of doing something they enjoy. They reclaimed their power, bit their own bullet, and broke free.

Many corporates I have known have turned to alcohol. They keep a bottle in their office drawer at work. Some of you may be able to relate to this. There is nothing wrong with doing this (as long as your workplace allows it), but when it becomes an escape from the corporate environment, you have created your own bullet.

It is no coincidence that the topics of well-being and mental health have become more dominant in the public domain at present. Many companies are finally recognising the importance of these for their employees. Offices in Canary Wharf provide yoga classes. This is all well and good, but biting your own bullet to achieve a state of relaxation is what's necessary, not just following a trend to incorporate yoga classes without the benefits they can bring to the state of mind of a corporate worker.

Biting your bullet will make your mind bulletproof. Any stresses you face on a daily basis will be like water off a duck's back. You have a lot of talent and potential.

The bright intern Moritz Erhardt, who died at the age of 21 in 2013 during a work placement scheme with a top bank in Central London, overworked himself. He was an overachiever throughout his academic life, and he was tipped for greatness. Mr Erhardt worked at many other top consulting companies/banks prior to joining this particular internship. Everyone noticed he was always working hard. Unfortunately, during a two-week period, he worked eight all-nighters. He would return home at six in the morning to shower and go back to work again. Mr Erhardt had lost himself and did not put himself first.

Mr Erhardt's imaginary bullet was the pressure to impress his bosses. He was only 21 and had a bright future ahead of him. He had such a strong mind during his studies, and he probably bit so many bullets throughout his school/college time that in a working environment, he lost himself to the corporates. The great gift he has left behind is a reminder to always love ourselves first before placing energy into something else. May his soul rest in peace. Thank you, Moritz, for making us aware of the potential dangers of losing ourselves.

Service men and women hold the most respect in terms of honour. There is a reason why they took on this role. People within this profession lose themselves as they put others first. This is a very honourable attribute, but losing themselves defeats the objective of why they entered the profession in the first place.

Consider the story of Dr Zhao Bianxiang. She worked in the Department of Respiratory Care at the Yuci District Hospital in Jinzhong, China. Dr Zhao was known as a workaholic and would never say no; even if she was not working, she would offer her assistance. Leading up to her death on 28 December 2017, Dr Zhao worked eighteen hours straight and eventually collapsed in front of a patient she was seeing. The cause of death was a rare type of stroke causing bleeding on the surface of the brain.

It was most likely not this one incident of Dr Zhao working eighteen hours straight that caused her death. It was most likely a number of years where Dr Zhao lost herself to her identity as a doctor. Continuously working overtime and not taking any breaks led to great stress placed upon herself and her mind. I have read that in China, 600,000 workers every year die by overworking themselves. These are examples of the bullet becoming an imaginary obligation of their job role.

The power to say no is your own power. Dr Zhao died at the age of 43 and was definitely very talented and a bright gift to this world, helping patients for many years. We thank Dr Zhao for the gift she has left the world, not just for the situation that led to her death but for the many patients she assisted throughout her career. May her soul rest in peace.

My cousin, who we shall call Gina, is in the police force and now at a senior rank. She has described to me some of the shocking incidents she has witnessed, whether attending the scene of a dead person, knife stabbings, or drug-related incidents. These can take a toll on the mental health of an individual, as these are not normal occurrences for you and I. Gina has a very strong mind and stepped into police work because she wanted to do something meaningful for society. She also has another job working in a medical research field.

Gina has asked herself the question of who she is and if she can be trusted. She knows herself and trusts herself. This removes imaginary bullets she has built for her mind and makes her bulletproof. The new chapter of her life is that now she is married. Gina has to continue staying strong mentally so that she does not lose herself in her new chapter. This is one person who definitely knows how to bite her own bullet anytime a situation may stand in her way.

My friend, who we shall name Guppy, is a nurse in a children's ward. Guppy left her sales job where she was earning good money after deciding that was not for her. I remember asking her at the time why she wanted a career change, and she stated that she wanted to do something meaningful and impactful for society. I have the utmost respect for her for making this decision to switch careers and taking this huge career step. She does not give herself enough credit for how she achieved that.

Guppy, prior to this, had gone through an emotional roller coaster where she split up with a partner she thought she would be with forever. They were together for six years, and she no longer had him in her life when they split. Reflecting back on this, Guppy grew a lot as a person from being out of that relationship. Her ways of thinking expanded, and she became a more conscientious person. This is probably what enabled her to look at the bigger picture of helping children who needed nursing back to health.

Guppy left the UK for two years and went to Australia to become a nurse. Her fitness blossomed whilst she was out there, and she was able to visit the beach daily to clear her mind. The fitness culture and well-being she was surrounded by was something Guppy needed, and it did her good. Her mind and body were becoming stronger.

I have advised Guppy to strengthen her mind, as she does not give herself enough credit for what she has been through and how she has come out of it. Guppy has since returned to the UK and brought with her the positive spirit she built up during her stay in Australia. After returning to the UK, she landed herself a job that she wanted, working in a very well-known children's hospital. She also met her current husband upon her return to the UK.

Guppy's example of decisiveness following a traumatic event has allowed her to excel in life. She often speaks to me of the challenges she faces. She is now entering a new chapter in her life where she is looking to bite another bullet to break free from her mind's imaginary scenarios. This new chapter is motherhood. Guppy is now a mother to her daughter.

We have seen many stories over the years of celebrities losing themselves. Elvis Presley and Amy Winehouse are two examples of losing themselves which led to their deaths. Drugs and alcohol were their escape from the pressure they both faced. There are many current celebrities who are thankfully still alive but have lost themselves in terms of achieving everything they had to achieve and feeling like they can offer nothing more. They do not know themselves. The belief and inner fire they once had has faded, and their bullet is feeling useless to society. This is far from true; if only they realised, they have many other gifts to share with the world.

Celebrities are human too. They encounter the same feelings as everyone else. The pressures they face from their agents, media, contractors, etc. diminishes their light and power. Celebrities who face this pressure must bite the bullet that stands in the way of reclaiming their power. They must find the courage to stand and say no in order to centre themselves before engaging in their next project.

We can be inspired by celebrities for their talents or for their message they project. But we must not lose ourselves when we idolise them and want to become exactly like them in an unhealthy manner. We must remain in our own power. The imaginary bullet we will create is one of constantly striving to become that celebrity. We must create our own path of who we want to be and what we want to offer to the world.

The elderly and retired can have a mindset somewhat similar to a celebrities. These are people who have been on the go for the majority of their life and are now in a position where they have to switch off and find something to occupy their lives. There are many opportunities they can take in terms of keeping themselves occupied to pursue their hobbies. But at this point in time, the decrease in attention will be somewhat alien to them. The strongest retired people are the ones who have given themselves new projects to tackle, such as DIY, attending the gym, travelling, and gardening.

How does one not lose oneself after retirement? The reigniting of passions or discovering a new passion may be the way. Why does this have to be a slowdown period of life? The talented Bob Proctor, an author and speaker known for his coaching and mentoring and a champion of success, is an excellent example of speeding up as he gets older. At the age of 85 (as of July 2019), Proctor is still sharp and has been pushing himself, as he has since the age of 26, to remain on the path of staying in tune with an abundance mindset. Any bullets that arise in his mind's eye he bites and makes them explode into energy for a future he creates.

Fauja Singh, the famous runner who took up running in his 80s after his wife passed away, had also lost his son to a horrific accident. One of his three daughters had also passed away. He is now 108 years old (as of March 2019). He has stated that after these traumatic events of loss, he slipped into depression. To bring himself out of it, he turned to running.

Singh has been running in marathons since the age of 80. At the age of 94, a test on his legs revealed that he had the bone density of a 25-year-old in his right leg and a 35-year-old in his left leg. Medical tests done at the age of 99 showed he had the fitness of a 40-year-old. This is a great example of a human being biting his own bullet after going through a traumatic event.

The key here for all of us who are yet to approach elderly life is to not wait too long in finding out who we are. The elderly have a better understanding of who they are, as they know themselves. For people in their late teens to 40s, we should get to know ourselves as soon as possible. Yes, it will change as the years go by, but the realisation in each of those stages is key to uprooting who we are and where we want to go. We will find that we are capable of achieving everything we want to achieve and more.

For parents, knowing who you are will enable you to realise who your children can become. It is not about knowing who they are right now. They are on their own journey. A parent's job is challenging, and many parents lose themselves as they put their kids first. This is normal and respectable.

It is also important to remember who you are. Think of being on an airplane, when the safety video or demonstration at the beginning of the flight says to secure your own oxygen mask first before securing your child's. The same thing applies to your child's journey to developing a bulletproof mind. Children look at their parents' actions for guidance. I'm sure you would want your child to have a bulletproof mind, but until you focus on your own state, it will be difficult to recognise the potential you can unleash from your child or children.

My sister Dee, who lives in San Diego with her husband and two kids, was trapped in an endless daily grind. I saw it for myself in October 2017 when I stayed with them for two weeks. My sister would wake up at 5:30 in the morning (maybe earlier) and get her two kids ready. She would then make them breakfast and drive them to school. Once that was done, she would make her way to work. During her working hours, there were many challenges in the environment she was working in. The good part was that she stayed within her power of challenging upwards and highlighting the toxic working environment with her boss. The team was not productive, and everyone was working in fear.

After working in this unhealthy atmosphere, my sister would come home and take her kids to after-school classes, whether it be maths tutorials, karate, etc. Once that was done, she would come home and cook dinner for the family. Don't get me wrong—her husband also did his share, picking up the kids up from school and helping around the house. But he also travelled for work in different states at times too.

Once my sister and her family ate, she would have a bit of time to spend talking with us, and then she would clean the kitchen. By this time, it would be eight o'clock or so. After that, she would be on her laptop doing more work for her boss. I would see her sitting at the table on her laptop feeling really drowsy as she cycled through work emails. On top of that, she would snack every now and again, and mainly on biscuits and such. At eleven o'clock, she was off to bed, and then back to the same cycle the following morning starting at five-thirty.

As an outsider looking in, I could see this was not healthy, either physically or mentally. My sister had lost herself. She was not biting her bullet. When she was at home and she would talk to her husband, the topic would be her work environment. There was no end to her cycle, and she needed to break out of it fast. The money was good, but the quality of life was not.

Since then, she has made the correct decision of biting her bullet, leaving that job, and not looking back. Financially, her husband was able to provide, and my sister was able to get to know herself again and really spend time with her kids. She had time to sense also that something was not right with her youngest daughter, whose energy was sluggish and health signs did not seem correct. Eventually, as my sister's maternal instincts kicked in, she took her youngest daughter to the hospital, and they found out she had type 1 diabetes. This can be looked at as a negative, but it's a positive in the sense that my sister was able to be present in this important time and spot the signs early. By biting her own bullet and removing that toxicity from her life, she was able to get to know herself and more about her family.

My sister is now working part-time, living a happier life, and spending time with her family. She is able to inspire others through her teaching and artwork. She is living her passions by taking up hobbies and teaching others dance and art, all the while allowing her children to live normal lives.

This is an example of biting your bullet and being strong enough to walk away from situations that do not serve you. The bullet in front of her all along was the fact that she felt she financially needed to keep the job. This was imaginary. What happened away from this situation was that she was able expand herself. Dee believed in herself and got to know herself. If she had continued the way she was headed, it could have led to a number of undesired outcomes. So well done, Dee.

Action Step: Knowing Yourself

To know yourself, you need to know where you are. Are you where you want to be, whether in your career or personal life or even in terms of items you would like to purchase? State where you are by describing your current lifestyle. Write down how your life is at present and the way it makes you feel. This actually brings to the forefront of your mind where exactly you are and surfaces any repressed feelings you may have about your current situation.

The following are generic examples:

- **Business owners**—Do you want to expand your business?
- **Students**—Where are you in terms of your academic knowledge?
- **Workers**—Where are you with your career ladder?
- **Those in relationships**—Do you know where the relationship is headed? List how the relationship is making you feel. If you are already in a long-term relationship, where are you now in terms of the quality of the relationship? Are you thinking of settling down in marriage with that person, or a civil partnership? If you both are not the marriage type, then is your plan to move in together?

There are many areas of your life you may wish to question, not just those above. For example, are you looking to improve your physique or general health goals? Regardless of your particular focus, by taking this step back, you are becoming aware of your current situation. The routine we are so accustomed to blurs where we are at present and causes us to pass up on the opportunity to analyse ourselves.

Are You Happy Where You Are?

Whether you have all your material possessions or not, are you happy with the relationships in your life? This is the deeper understanding we want behind this question. Even wealthy people may be unhappy, sometimes through loneliness. Happiness within is extremely important for living the quality life we desire.

There was a programme about a father in India from the villages who had bills to pay and kids to put through school. A street seller, he had a limited amount of stock to sell on a daily basis, such as food items. He was very successful in selling out every day. A question was posed to him about expanding his business, and he declined. He sold what he had and returned home. That was his daily target, and he had no need to expand.

There are many like this gentleman who live the same way. They are not striving for extra material possessions. The contented way they live every day is enough to keep them happy. These contented people are truly happy, as they know themselves. Hats off to them. They are able to provide their children the paid education they need without struggling.

Are You Living the Life You Want?

This is different from happiness. The man above with the food business in India is living the life he wants. Others may have a mansion with the type of car they would like to drive, and they are living the life *they* want. So what about you?

If you are a student, are you living the life you want? Take into account your social circles. Are your friends holding you back in any way? How do you actually feel around them? Are you not getting your work done at home because you are pleasing them more than you are paying attention to yourself? How does that make you feel?

To the worker, are you living the life you want with the job that you have? You could be a part-time worker with kids, and this suits your lifestyle. However, there may be other passions you would like to pursue or create outside of that bubble to be living the life you want. This does not necessarily mean you are unhappy. You can be happy and want to achieve more. The other end of the spectrum is, are you living the life you want if you are unhappy with your current financial situation or current relationships?

What Action Steps Have You Taken to Change Your Current Situation?

Against your list of the above, evaluate whether you have taken action on anything about those items before. This reminder is great to get you into a realisation process of what kind of action you should take. Are your thoughts controlling you, or are you allowing your current situation to control you?

Taking a step back to analyse your actions will highlight who are you in terms of allowing it to happen or making it happen. It is a very simple step yet very effective. This is my favourite one, as it is all about action and showing ourselves whether we are creating change.

Do You Have Any Regrets from the Past?

This is highly important and probably one of the most important steps to creating a strong belief in yourself and your abilities. Regrets are a vibration we should never have to revisit. It is easier said than done, but you cannot change the past. Take the time to look at any regrets you have had in life, whether it be letting an ex get away, letting your money go to waste on things that did not serve you in the long run, or not contacting a close family member or friend over a small matter that pushed you apart.

Any deep regrets you have, recall them. The worst thing we can do is hide them deep within ourselves. The strong bulletproof mind does not look back. Therefore, realising that you have regrets is important in tending to the garden of your mind. You want to pull out the weeds, which do not serve your flourishing nature.

Recognise your regrets. Cry them out if you have to, but don't ignore them. They are there as a message to heal yourself and move forward. To be a truly inspirational and great leader of yourself and others, bite your bullet and confront your silenced side. Feel your strength of character and become the confident warrior you truly are. Others around you will feel this. I urge you to delve deep into your mind and confront your regrets.

Action Step: What Do You Think About on a Daily Basis?

This is important. Regretful thoughts can always pop up in our daily thinking. However, if you are getting into your car in the morning and you say to yourself, "I can't be bothered to go into work today," that is a thought you need to write down or make a note of on your phone. Keeping a log of your thoughts throughout the day will assist in identifying what is it you think about.

Most of the thoughts we have throughout the day are not remembered. The speed of thought is the fastest thing in the known universe. Speed of light is not as quick as the speed of thought. Therefore, if you can catch your thoughts, you will become a mastermind of how your thoughts shape your reality.

Where Do You Want to Be?

This is the positive change we want to see in our lives. No one is going to write down, "I want to be miserable and be worried and anxious about my future wealth and relationships." This is your chance to shift the focus of your life. Do you want to be financially stable, in a loving relationship, a confident leader, a homeowner, a student passing with the best grades? Do you want to start a family or take up new hobbies? This is all about you. You are at centre stage when it comes to your life and where you want to be.

Note that I said *want* to be, not *need* to be. You are the one who is envisioning the lifestyle you would like to be living at present. How about your fitness goals? Do you want to eat nutritious foods? How about your physique? Do you want to work out to get the body you desire? You can be a worker and just simply want to be the best at what you do. Once you reach that goal, you will find the confidence to reevaluate where you want to be and want something even more thereafter. There are endless possibilities.

Action Step: List It!

You have rooted out the questions deep within. Any bullets you have identified are now evident in your conscience mind. Where do you want to go? Do you believe you can get there?

If you believe you can't, don't feel embarrassed or ashamed. This is just a measure of where your mind is. It does not define who you are as a person. This is purely identifying your belief in yourself. And it's a win in itself if you are for the first time addressing it by holding up this mirror in front of you, so be as brutally honest as you can.

If you believe in yourself and have no unwavering thoughts about moving forward, then great. Keep that momentum and energy going. Both answers are wins.

If you answered no to your abilities, then that's still great. You are making yourself aware, and you can work towards sharpening those abilities.

Write down all of the questions in this chapter and answer them. See what you come up with. This is the starting point to recognising who you are.

Conclusion

All of the real-life examples above are mirrors I am holding up in front of you, regardless of who you are and what stage of life you are in. Looking into other lives and considering where you can end up—both desired and undesired—should allow you to realise how important you really are and how much you are controlled by imaginary bullets. If you are happy to be working where you are, this is great. If you are happy with the relationship you are in, that is great—as long as you don't lose your own sense of power. That sense is far more valuable to the world as a whole and to your relationships. By believing in and knowing yourself, you are able to give better quality to your relationships, including family, lovers, friends, and work colleagues.

People want to be around people who know themselves and the world around them. Think how you feel in the presence of people who are unsure of themselves and view situations as negative all the time. The draining feeling you get is not an illusion; it is the energy given off by that person.

Think about singers or a live orchestra. The energy they put into their performance can be felt by the audience. If they did not believe in themselves and their performance, this would be felt by all in attendance as something flat.

Hold on to the list of answers you have made to the questions above. These should act as a reminder moving forward and will definitely be revisited as we move towards the bulletproof mind.

CHAPTER 2

The Oxymoron of the Comforting Bullet

A comforting bullet sounds rather strange. But constantly having our goals blocked because of an excuse keeps us in our daily routines. This can be running a PB in a certain time, building your own furniture, starting your own business, drawing something for the first time, or diving from a swimming board. Striving for targets can seem out of reach if all you have ever known is *average* or *not possible*.

Targets at work, for example, can seem impossible if you don't have a supportive leader above you. If you are feeling under pressure from your boss at work as opposed to being coached and developed, it is easy to feel all the pressure pile up on you. Your boss is one element, but the main element is you. If you have no belief that you can obtain a particular target, you have already lost and given up before getting started. A winning mentality is highly important.

There was a store I managed for a fashion company that had many problems. It was considered a *red store*—a problem store. The basics of organisation were not in place. The team members were not getting on with each other. There were suspicions of internal theft by certain team members. All this chaos going on this was the reason the store was in that particular state. Ultimately, customers were affected by this.

Upon arrival at the store, I had the firm belief that it could be the best store. I spoke with the deputy manager on the phone prior to arriving, and she explained that she and another member of management were not seeing eye to eye. On my first meeting with my deputy, I stated, "We'll be the best store with the best results."

Her response to me was, "I'm the type of person that when I see it, I believe it." She was sceptical.

We did end the year with one of the best results in the company for sales target growth. The comforting bullet the store had was the same atmosphere day in and day out. There was no positivity in the store team, and this was what they had become accustomed to. Within three months, I was able to change the team mentality to a winning mentality. I would constantly highlight to the whole team the importance of being the best store. The atmosphere created rippled across to the team that my expectation as the leader of the store was that we would be the best.

The journey was not totally straightforward, although in my head, I had no other thought but success. It wasn't simply about me being positive and happy. That was the fuel that inspired the team but not the only action taken. There were many targets to be achieved, also known as key performance indicators (KPIs). These KPIs ranged from sales targets, stock loss (the store had high theft), customer service, and staff retention.

Surveys in which customers left feedback regarding their experience were a vital element, as these addressed the public's impression of the store. The comforting bullets long-time team members had about the surveys included the following:

- "Customers don't want to fill out the survey."
- "I keep trying, but then I never get any feedback, so I stopped." (Customers had the option to mention the name of the person who served them, which is how we would know who received the feedback.)
- "We have never done this before."
- "I think it's pointless. I know I give good customer service."

Newer team members fresh into their roles were achieving on this KPI. The older members of the team were able to adapt after seeing the possibilities.

When I arrived at that particular store, the customer feedback count for the month was six. This was with a team of forty people in total working there. The average of the store should have been twenty-five to thirty. Once the team was reset and got into the flow of receiving feedback, we were one of the best stores, with a count of forty to fifty on average per month. It had been proven already to my deputy that on the customer KPI, we were able to get away from receiving only six feedback responses.

Simple steps to change the atmosphere, such as cleaning all the back areas of the store for staff to work in a clean environment and also cleaning the staff room, assisted in a full change of atmosphere. When I first suggested this to the deputy, she was quite defensive about all the changes taking place. When I pointed to the results a few months later, she was not extremely happy, even though everything in the store was improving tenfold.

The comforting bullet the deputy had developed over her year and a half working there prior to my arrival was one of negativity and low performance. She had become comfortable with this, and as strange as it sounds, found this negativity comfortable and acceptable. Thankfully, as time went on, she caught on to the buzz of the winning mentality. She could see the rest of the stores acknowledging our store's results and achievements.

This is an example of how team members can feel comfortable with their surroundings and routine of negative results. Look at your own life, whether it be work-related or personal. What is it you are accepting and finding comfortable? It could be something as small as a broken picture frame on your wall. It is easy to get used to these things you see every day.

The comforting part that I want us all to have a look at is the fact that feeling like you cannot change your outcome becomes a normal expectation within. This is the oxymoron of the comforting bullet. The fact the bullet remains in front of you and hinders your progress can be comforting too. Change disrupts our comfort zone. Whenever I approached a store, I would bring in change to the whole environment.

The spark you create yourself will bring about a natural shift in your environment, no matter where it is. This must be done authentically, with genuine positive feelings behind your actions. Positivity does not mean you have to be airy-fairy and happy. I'm talking about positivity in the sense of a *can do, will do* attitude. This leads the way for others to see the possibilities.

Change management is talked about in many companies, and is true to an extent. There are many phased changes. It should never mean that you slow down in how you would like to approach a situation to bring winning changes, however. Change management and working with self-belief to impact your environment with winning results is the best change of spirit you can bring to your teams. If you take the long haul and approach it hesitantly, you will only become another corporate.

Add the feeling and personable approach with passion in accordance with a plan. A winning mentality travels across the team as the expectation of being the best is felt everywhere. But this must be done without forcing team members to change. It is done in a more inspiring way.

Another friend of mine, who I will name Amber, went through a phase of purchasing designer handbags, which cost almost £500 or more per piece. She would often state that she wanted to save money, yet she would make these lavish purchases. The spending spree was her comfort. Now Amber looks back on her spending days and realises the amount of money she would have saved had she not spent so lavishly.

At that particular time, spending money was Amber's comfort zone, and the bullet she had created was a spending mentality and not one of saving. This is a real example of being comfortable with your bullet. If she did not want to change and was spending in this manner, that was her choice to live with. But the main point she brought up was that she *wanted to save*.

Action Step: What Are Your Comforting Bullets?

What are you comfortable with at this moment in your life that is going unnoticed that you would like to change? Write it down.

What are the habits you have in your life that you often reflect upon that you would like to change? If you have not reflected on anything, then this is the time to do so. Write it down.

For example, do you reach for the biscuit jar every day when you have the intention that you want to eat more fruit and veg? Has this become a normal routine for you every day after you come home from work or school, that you feel like binge snacking? Do you wish to spend more time on your hobbies, but then social media takes over more of your time as you become distracted by things popping up on your social feed?

Do you rush out of the house every morning and always wish you had more time to eat breakfast, when you know that waking up fifteen minutes earlier can assist you in having a smooth transition for your whole morning and in fact whole day ahead, as you would have had breakfast? From personal experience, I know how alert and calm I feel when I have had breakfast in a non-hurried manner. Before, if I had breakfast and rushed my eating, it would assist me in terms of having fuel for the day, but mentally I was still in a rushed state, which would branch out through to my whole day. Many people I have worked with feel the same way; they are more focussed once they have prepared themselves for the day with fuel.

Identify and write down areas where you have this comforting bullet facing you. List actions you can take that would break this cycle and make the bullet disappear. Use the example that follows as a format for how to write it:

> I have a gym membership but have not been going for a month. When I come home after work, I am too tired to go back out to attend the gym. This has been my comfort zone, as I sit down on the sofa and don't feel

like getting back up. *Be really honest with yourself and blunt as possible to trigger this in you.*

Actionable solutions

- If driving: I'll pack my gym clothes in my bag and keep them in the car and attend gym straight after work.
- If travelling by public transport: find a gym close to where I work, take a gym bag with me to work, then go straight after work.

Planning steps

I'll start off small, maybe thirty mins a day for two weeks and see how I feel and if I would like to increase it. At minimum, I will go for four days a week, just basic running on the treadmill and light weights.

Or I don't even need a gym membership. I can run around my area for twenty minutes, then come home and do my free weights and sit-ups/press-ups.

The above is simply a starting point. You can expand on this as much as you like. If you would like to incorporate gym programmes and classes, you can include those in there too.

The main reason for doing this task is to get motivated in making a start. When you start listing the action steps towards your desired outcome, you are able to see the possibilities, feel them coming together, and be inspired to stick to your action plan.

The main message of this chapter is that although it is called a comforting bullet, it is destroying your progress. Bite it.

CHAPTER 3

What Goals Do You Have?

When you take a bite of your bullet, you become the bullet. What happens when you become this bullet? You begin to move at the speed of a bullet, and in one forward direction.

A bullet never returns to the barrel of the gun once a shot has been fired. Move forward, my friend, and you won't have to care what is behind you because you are so far ahead. Razor-sharp confidence will be flowing through your mind and body. Those who are in touch with their soul level will feel the energy resonate through them with a sense of knowing.

Action Step: List the Goals You Would Like to Achieve

Questions to assist you in getting your brain in gear are as follows:

- Are your grades in school/college/uni where you need them to be?
- Do you want to change jobs?
- Do you want a promotion?
- Do you want to get into a relationship?
- Do you like your body shape?
- Are you pushing the strongest weight you can at the gym?
- Do you want to open your own business?

The above questions are examples of how you are able to set yourself goals by questioning your environment. Day to day, it is very easy to get lost in the environment we are in.

Many people are deterred by the goals they set. The goal-setting mentality can be quite exhausting, as you want to deliver on promises to yourself without any failure. It becomes easy to avoid the goals you set and make up excuses for not accomplishing them.

A common example can be seen with fitness/weight-loss goals. There is a lot of emotional and mental stress around them. The common pattern seen is discouragement over the length of time it takes for weight to come off. It is helpful to learn how weight loss occurs: for example, that it takes more than thirty minutes of cardio to burn fat or that water gets released from the body first, then fat cells begin to shrink. Most people, when weighing in, get short-term happiness seeing that they have lost weight on the scale, but they are disappointed a week later when they have gained two or three pounds, as it was only water they lost from their body.

Knowing which foods to eat to prevent weight gain and having a calorie deficit is another educating step for someone who wants to lose weight. This knowledge preparation is something that mentally prepares you for the journey ahead. A goal should be considered a journey, as opposed to something you hit instantly. This is where disappointment can begin.

The example above is about weight loss, but you can apply it to anything. Let's take money-saving. The discipline required to save money can be alien to people at first. The budget-setting is a starting point, where a person makes a commitment to save £200 per month as an example. For the people who can stick to savings, this is great.

If you are one of those people who goes off track sometimes, what is it that you are spending your money on? Spending the money you have in your bank account provides a rush, almost like an addiction to spending. It is comforting when you have the money in your account and can spend it as you wish. It is like a loaded weapon. What I have found is that when you have no reason to save money, this is when the spending begins. The bullet that is created for those who love to spend when they should be saving has to do with a longing for freedom. I have been there in the past. I would spend whatever I wanted, because I had no goal.

I discovered discipline when I was saving to buy a house. The goal I had set for myself was something I firmly believed in, and I would target how much I wanted to save per month. At the time, though, when it came to purchasing a house, there were many temptations to purchase something else—such as a car or holidays—as I had saved a healthy amount at that particular time. Discipline becomes very important for reminding yourself why you have saved that money.

The bullet that can be created by spending is a sense of false freedom, a sense of power and control. Think of your money as energy. The energy it took for you to create and receive that money is a quantifiable number for you. Where you wish to spend your money is where you wish to expel your energy.

Look at it from the point of view of energy, and you will think twice before transferring your energy into a pint of beer or a chocolate you have just seen in the petrol station or that £6 coffee (slight exaggeration) when that energy can go into your goal of saving for something big like a house, wedding, study funds, or anything that requires a large amount. A budget can be set for the beer, chocolate, and coffee, where you feel even more in control of your spending on these impulses. Call it an impulse budget.

The bullets we create can definitely be bitten. Focus on why you want to achieve a certain goal. When you lose focus, you have to be strong enough to remind yourself of why you have embarked on that particular path of achievement. What has made you focus on the goal in the first place, and what benefits will this be bringing you?

What Is the Formula for Achieving Your Goal?

My purpose for writing this book is that I have a strong sense that my achievements in my career and personal life are gifts that should be shared. The gift I am speaking of is the "never stop" mentality I possess.

My testing ground has always been my workplace and managing a team in retail. Retail management is dynamic and ever-changing. You are challenged physically, mentally, and at times emotionally.

If you do not work in retail, here is a picture for you of what happens and why it differs from office work or non-customer-facing roles. The team environment is made up of many different personalities and age groups. Work-shift patterns can vary from early morning to late night depending on when people are available to work to suit their lifestyles. Mums come and work at certain times, students, people who have two jobs, or people dedicated to progression. The variations in personality dynamics are endless.

Why is this worth mentioning? It places an importance on how connected a leader of the team has to be and how relatable a leader must be towards each member's personality and energy. That energy will vary from person to person and day to day. A student who is stressed out about exams and coming to work to assist the store with targets has to be motivated in a different way. The mum who has left her child with a carer or a friend to look after has to think about other variables, such as feeding her kids and completing other chores. The mum has to be motivated in a different way. The good thing is, once you set the motivational tone, everyone begins to become self-motivated, and they know the expectation thereafter.

On top of managing people's schedules of different availability criteria, a leader interacts with customers too. You can enjoy your job and face a variety of customers. I have witnessed colleagues having to put on a customer-facing personality when they can be having the most awful time in their personal lives. This is something that has to be commended. You can't hide behind a phone. Sometimes stressed customers have been known to get heated at staff members.

Physically, you see the team working to move objects around, remerchandising a shop floor to make it easy for customers to navigate and enjoy their shopping journey. Mentally, you see them dealing with targets (KPIs) set by the head office, which stores must strive to reach in order to meet the company's goal of growth. Emotionally, you see employees who are affected by home life or the pressure of keeping up with the job. On top of this, the whole team has personal moments outside of work which can potentially affect them emotionally.

This, in a nutshell, is how a store operates, whether it be a fashion clothing store, sportswear store, DIY, supermarket, etc. My calling came through target-achieving. The main reason for targets for any company is growth. Targets for yourself in your personal life are also for growth. A company has a requirement for growth, and if the store achieves it, that is a win for the company. The workers who achieve the target may receive a bonus for it, and that is a win for them.

When the store and company achieve their targets, ultimately the customer wins, as the service satisfaction is met. This can involve behind-the-scenes activity which the customer does not see. Stockrooms and warehouses have targets too. This ultimately benefits customers through organisation and efficiency of stock. The better-organised a store is, the more efficiently it serves the customer.

When I was a supervisor in 2008, my store manager at the time challenged me on a certain target for the store. We had to promote a credit card. I was 23 at the time, and I did not even have a credit card at that age. The target for the store was to sign up ten customers for cards per day.

One particular day, I had gone to the upper floor of the building, which was where the manager's office was located. My manager at the time was a very challenging lady we shall call Pearl. Pearl was a character who was very vocal about her feelings if she was unhappy. She was very competitive and pushed her results to always strive for the best.

Pearl asked me at that moment, "Vijay, how many cards are we on?"

I replied, "Six. Most people are saying they don't want one."

The reply I received from Pearl was as follows: "For fuck sake, Vijay."

I was not offended, nor was I upset, but I *was* quite surprised that it meant that much to her. That day marked the start of my winning mentality for career-based targets. It was my turning point or whatever you wish to call it. How you perceive a situation can make or break you. In that moment, my attitude was to be a winner. I did not do it for my manager, although I grew to respect her. I did it for myself.

My accountability in that situation became leading the shop floor team to strive to achieve this credit card target. I took on a persona of a warrior, and instead of shying away from this target, I engrossed myself in it. I wanted to find out how the card worked; I became a student of this card. The team could see I was passionate about achieving this target for the store, and the buy-in from the team was that they wanted to get involved.

I did not realise this at the time, as I was involved with leading and being in in the present moment. Then I noticed that the team would actively speak about the targets we had met and communicate that to me. I would encourage them to bring out the warrior side of themselves too. Funny enough, on a side note, I introduced an award called "Vj'z Weekend Warrior"!

What resulted from this was that I became well known within the London region regarding the credit card. Conference calls were hosted by the regional manager (Pearl's boss), and I would initiate a competition with the managers from other stores. At the time, I was a supervisor, and they were all store managers. I would feed off this winning mentality. In the car on the way to work, I would say out loud, "Today we will open ten credit cards." I remember one day telling Pearl we had reached the target. I told her that I had said to myself in the car that morning that we would achieve that amount.

Sundays were the start of the week, and the Sunday conference call was very lively. Team members from different stores would take part. As I challenged all of the stores on who would be the best store, my name would eventually get chanted on the call by the largest store in London, Oxford Street.

Finally, the biggest honour for me at the time, which I am proud reflecting upon, was that I was appointed to host the conference call for the credit card target. I was very happy to do this. I was operating with no fear and enjoying this company target and responsibility.

Coming back to Pearl and the situation where she shouted at me: I had created my own bullet of accepting the reality of customers stating they did not want to open a card. But this was far from true. There were customers who wanted this card, as it would help with their credit rating to get a loan in the future or purchase a car or house. This barrier I had created for myself was limiting my growth.

Of course, if there is a target, you expect to have challenging steps in the way. It is how you overcome them that will define your attitude. Over the past fifteen years, I have worked with managers who would give up at the first hurdle and use this as an excuse to not push for targets. I, on the other hand, looked at it as an opportunity to grow and find a way to achieve. I can tell you many approaches to use in achieving your goals, but the will to succeed at anything has to come from the individual. I can inspire you with all the successes I have had in different aspects of my life on top of my personal goals, all whilst new ones are created.

If you want to succeed in your career or personal goals, you need an attitude of finding ways to achieve that will push you forward and give you that bulletproof confidence. The best part about this is the moment you change. You will get resistance from colleagues or people around you who will notice you behaving differently, and it will make them uncomfortable when they question you on how you are behaving. That is not your burden to take on.

What I have witnessed in these situations is that people looking to make positive growth changes in their life get questioned by people around them. This questioning deters individuals from progressing, as they feel silly for thinking positively and then discourage themselves, in the process creating a bullet.

I have to give you that push to discard any negativity or barriers in your way. Whether it is your best friend, cousin, work colleague, parent—if someone is questioning why you are changing into something else, you must know it is for a win-win situation for growth. Ultimately, when you're growing and achieving, the people around you will benefit off this energy as well. You have to believe in yourself that you are doing the right thing.

How Can You Believe in Yourself?

The way to believe in yourself is simple: create a framework of how and when you will make time for your goals, and then keep at it consistently. In chapter 9, you will find a timetable that you can replicate. Why does this create the believing-in-yourself mentality? It is because you are finally making time to make the change.

Many people dream of achieving and leave it at that. How many times at the beginning of the new year are you pumped up that you want to achieve your goal, and six months later you have not even started, yet alone achieved? It is common to make excuses of work taking up too much time or social commitments taking over, but I do not believe in these. When you see the timetable in chapter 9, you will see for yourself that it is possible to make time for what you want to achieve. This is how you create belief in yourself.

There is one relative of mine who we shall call Sigmund. He was approaching age 40, and he was married with two kids. Sigmund wanted to complete a university degree. He would not be seen at social events with the family on certain weekends, as he was at home studying for his degree. He was already in a well-paid job in finance, but this was something personal to him which he wanted to achieve. We did not know he was studying for a degree until one day he announced to everyone that he had passed with a first honours degree. He celebrated this with a party that he threw with all the family to celebrate his achievement.

My point in highlighting Sigmund's story is that our family is very committed to social events, and there is always a large turnout. Sigmund made the decision to make time for himself, and on weekends, when he was not working, he disciplined himself to focus on the goal at hand. He even reduced his alcohol consumption at this point, and he does enjoy a drink. Sigmund bit his bullet of excuses, and this gave him the energy and motivation to stay focussed on his degree completion. He created a firm belief in himself.

When you are fixated on achieving your goals, you automatically cut down on any other distractions. You have to do it to feel what I am talking about. Until you attempt to act, you will see everything as words and a dream.

Believing in yourself is the biggest battle you will face. When I passed my motorcycle test, for example, that was a confirmation that I had achieved. During the training sessions of learning how to ride a motorcycle, you know whether you are performing. The validation from the instructor gives you confirmation that you are moving in the right direction.

When I wanted to purchase a house, seeing the money I was putting in savings each month accumulate in the bank account was a confirmation to myself that I was heading in the correct direction. Further research allowed me to see how I could put the money towards purchasing a house. These steps forward encouraged me to stay on track.

The biggest challenge in my life has been my body physique. You don't notice the results straight away when working on your physical appearance. Even if you are lifting weights heavier than before, you are not seeing the changes as quickly as you would like. Patience was something I had to learn. It is easy to be deterred from continuing, as you are thinking you are doing all you can and still there is no change.

The bullet I had created for myself at this point was "quick result." The quick result mentality meant I was not valuing myself. Thinking about a flower and its journey through time, there is a certain amount of growth required to achieve an end goal. When it comes to body improvements, whether weight loss or improving the physique, others around you will begin to notice, but you yourself will not see it as suddenly as others.

This has been my greatest learning with the body goal, and I love the fact that something where you see yourself every day and do not notice the change is the biggest challenge you can place against yourself. You can overcome this challenge by being consistent with your body goal and taking pictures to demonstrate your month-by-month improvement. This is where your mind becomes even more bulletproof as you begin to believe and achieve.

The Battle of the Heart and Mind

The biggest battle you will face in any of your goals is the battle of the heart and mind. Your mind can be focussed on the goal at hand. Your heart can be putting everything into it. Then, when you're feeling tired, your mind may want to encourage you to abandon your goal whilst the heart says to continue. This constant battle of the heart and mind is one you must pay attention to in order to believe in yourself.

This is where placing value upon yourself happens. If you have been working towards your goal for a long time and you feel ready to give up, take a step back and reward yourself with a rest. You are allowed to rest. With body-building or fitness goals, rest is actually important. If one of your goals is to learn to play a new instrument, then the mental practice needed for learning requires rest too. When you reward yourself with rest by not attempting to practice for one or two days and then return to practice, it is almost like magic that you are able to play better.

What does it mean when you take steps such as these? It means you believe in yourself and enjoy the talent you are developing. None of this is dreamlike. It is actually real. When you realise you're capable of anything, the belief within you grows, and you are pumped up to try as many new things as possible. This is how self-belief is built, and when consistent, it creates confidence. If you are a leader of a team, they will feel your confidence and look up to you. You'll also be encouraging them to better themselves on a daily basis.

Look at yourself in the mirror up close, look straight into your eyes, and say these words to yourself: *You are very powerful* You will feel the belief, and the reason why you will feel the belief is because it is true. The close eye contact is very surreal and inspiring when you are talking positively to yourself.

The Golden Bullet

Ultimately, I viewed the targets set by the companies I worked for as a win-win, for both the company and the customers. Some customers have the perception that staff members only promote certain products as a way to achieve their targets. They feel "sold to" and devalued. Customers want to win too. The intention of the leaders in any field should be to promote a win-win mentality.

The golden bullet mentality is to push forward for yourself and your team. Reflect back on a time or multiple times you have become golden. It can be in anything from personal to work life. You will be surprised, when you think about the times you have succeeded at something, by how it benefited those around you, creating that win-win outcome.

Maybe you built a shed and the whole family benefited from it. Passed your driving test? This can benefit family and friends, since now you are able to assist them with travel if they need it. You may be a parent changing your lifestyle to make healthier food choices, and your kids have copied your lead. You may have given up smoking, a win-win for your body and the example you set for those around you.

CHAPTER 4

Confidence-Building

This chapter is the most important to me, and it marks the turning point in many people's lives. For me, confidence is the foundation of everything in life, and my only wish for the world is for every individual to feel confident. The biggest thing I have learnt in life so far is that a lot of people wish they could be more confident at something or take that big step from which something has always held them back. That something is a lack of self-confidence.

If you cannot immediately do the tasks suggested in this chapter due to location, then please ensure you make time for yourself to complete them later. I would encourage you to keep a file of all the papers you are going to use, as these will be an investment you are making in yourself. If you are confident already, use these activities to sharpen your confidence tools further.

I have encountered people who appear to be really confident with what they have achieved, only to find through conversation that they get nervous in public speaking or situations where they are put on the spot. There are those who have accomplished so much in life they have used success to avoid their deep traumas and live through their ego. The danger of living through the ego is that one day, the layers fade away and expose an individual who is potentially lonely and suffering.

There is something to improve on for us all, no matter what our level of confidence may be. There are others I have encountered who I thought were very confident, but they did not feel it. Out of fear, they reacted to situations in a loud manner, but really on the inside they were forcing themselves to be loud. For these types of personalities, faking it is fine, but the moment there is resistance from someone or a stab at them, their confidence dwindles. We want true confidence, where you can have a natural response and feel centred when encountering difficult situations.

Becoming Confident

Gaining confidence is easy, I promise you. I have been told many times that I am confident, and I have never been aware of what exactly people have meant by that. For many years, I thought everyone was the same. You have to remember, as a kid, I was confident in certain areas but not all of them, and it was not true confidence. I was only confident in my comfort zones. Encouraging kids to gain confidence through self-expression is a responsibility parents and teachers need to take seriously.

Many times throughout my life and career, I have heard the word *confidence*: confidence to speak up, confidence to perform in sports, confidence to perform onstage, confidence in yourself, confidence in others, a confident person, a confident leader. *Confidence* and *confident* are very powerful words, as they encompass belief and faith in an individual's character. To understand the journey of how an individual can be confident, I look at my own journey first.

Up until the age of 10, I was not so confident. What I mean by that is I would not speak up around certain people. Then, for some reason, I began finding a new confidence in my personality, and that was through football and karate.

I remember to this day when I was sitting on the school wall with a girl from my class and speaking to her about how I was not good at football. I don't know where this came from, but I think it all came down to my confidence level at the time. I always used to be in goal, as I found that my comfort area. The root cause of my confidence growing now came from expression.

This is what I can say for everyone too. Your talents do not make you a confident person. Your expressive self is what will make you become confident, as you are being true to yourself and giving yourself the ability to develop your talent even further. How beautiful it is to know that your true self is all you need to become confident, as that means you are just being you.

Back to the story: I started hanging out with a different set of friends when going out after school. This groups was a bit more on edge compared to the people I was hanging out with before. They were a bit of a bad influence, in the sense that two of them, who were age 10 at the time like me, were smoking cigarettes. Thankfully I did not get involved with that, but I still considered them my friends, as they did not force me to smoke. This I believe had a massive impact on my character overall, as I became more expressive. What happened was that in class, I would be more vocal about things I liked and disliked when speaking with my teachers.

After always being in goal for football, when I was playing football outside of school with my new set of friends, I started to play out of goal. Within one evening, I discovered I was very good at playing football away from goal. Overnight, I became the best football player in my class. The kids in the year above me were watching me play too, and they were shocked at what I was doing. For some reason, I was not shocked. I was just playing freely.

The whole point of this story is to highlight the root of my confidence. This new expressive way I discovered was the catalyst to making the decision to step out of my comfort zone of playing in goal. I was being expressive with my feelings in class, and I was becoming a leader by following my own set of beliefs. The teachers noticed this, and many of my classroom peers noticed this as well. The only negative point is I became a little disruptive to the class due to all this newfound attention, but I was a kid, so I forgive myself for being like that.

Increasing your confidence level is all about how free you are to express yourself. I am glad I learnt this at an early age, and I feel really blessed by this. I was able to carry this forward to high school and college, where I even took up acting modules in drama.

If you want to unlock your children's confidence levels, you must allow them to become expressive, not only at home but also outside of home. Kids who are expressive at home and quiet outside find home too comfortable. Think of children who do not want to leave their parent's side when they are outside of the home; it is because of the comfort they feel. Kids need to be encouraged to express themselves as much as possible. If they have a talent or skill, we should encourage them to get better at what they are doing. This is unlocking their expressive side.

Fast forward now into our adult years. I have come across many people who are too afraid to talk in a WhatsApp group, as they fear what other people in the group may think when they say something. In the meditation group I attend, there is one lady who we will name Suzy. We have a WhatsApp group where, after each session, those who attended share their experience. Suzy came to the meditation sessions for the first few weeks. When she was asked why she did not share her experience on the WhatsApp group, she said she felt self-conscious.

I was highly amazed at this, as I thought the sharing was something so easy to do. I did appreciate that what is small to one person may seem big to another. Suzy was 55 years old and still felt like she couldn't express herself after all those years. She went on to explain that she felt shy in many situations and not just in a WhatsApp group. She stated that at parties, she would often feel like this. Alcohol helped her become more expressive.

If you find yourself low on confidence for whatever reason, what bullet have you created for yourself? I am extremely passionate about encouraging everyone to become confident, as it is your true self to be confident. No one should feel small around other people because they feel they are not allowed to express themselves. The energy you have inside you is to be shared with the world. If you have gone through hard times in the past and this has had a knock on your confidence, it is time to address this.

The world needs leaders. Leaders are confident even when they don't want to be. Anyone can be a leader. Leaders lead leaders too, so there is always an abundance of leaders available. There does not have to be only one.

Action Step: Analysing Your Lack of Confidence

Here is what needs to happen: if you are low on confidence, analyse which situations you feel really small in.

- Is it at work?
- Is it at social gatherings?
- Is it when you drive?
- Is it during sports contests?
- Is it during speaking in front of others?
- Is it when you are alone?

The above are just a few examples, and I appreciate that we each have our own journey regarding how expressive we want to be. This does not mean that if you are a quiet person generally, you are not a confident person. There are many people who are calm and collected and can be confident in expressing themselves when they need to.

Where people need to express themselves is when they are not comfortable with a situation. That sort of thing can fester if we try to ignore it. Handling it in a responsive way is always best. The reactive way of blowing up with emotion, such as anger, is not the correct way either; you lose your power, and this goes against your confidence. You have allowed another person to affect you to the point where you lose yourself to extreme anger.

If you are angry at a situation, it is perfectly fine to feel that anger. That is a signal from your body that you are not in agreement with what is taking place. Your job is to address that with yourself first as to why you are feeling like that, and then with the other person. If you do not have the courage to speak up about how you are feeling, this will always be a bullet stopping you from being your true self. Your true self is perfect. The evolution of your skill set is for you to keep flowing with your skills and prevent yourself from becoming stagnant.

Your Attitude

Before we get into the attitude of work, what is *attitude*? This word to me is one of the most important and can be applied to all aspects of our lives, work or personal. For me, the word describes how we perceive a situation and act according to the reality we have created. The perceptions we have lead the way to how we live our lives.

For example, what is your attitude towards public transport, such as the bus? One attitude is that they are late, unsafe, expensive, never on time, and too cold or too hot depending on season. Another attitude can be one of gratitude for the following:

- a bus service that can take you from one destination to another in a way that's less stressful than driving in traffic
- the driver whose job it is to allow you to travel
- the bus lane as a dedicated lane for buses, which someone actually thought to create

The second attitude displays more appreciation for the bus.

Certain students in the world have to walk three miles to go to school. Even though that does not affect you, can you imagine their attitude towards a bus service taking them to school daily? The students would find so much value in this. Their attitude towards their education is very appreciative of anything that assists them. Learning is something not to complain about in the reality they have created.

The first attitude highlights situations heard by many people we may know and some of you reading this. The solution is in the problem. For example, consider the idea that the bus is always late. The bulletproof mind will alter this to consider what we can do if this is the case. Ideas include leaving home fifteen minutes earlier to catch the earlier bus, or writing to the transport service that the buses are always late (if that really is the case).

If the bus really is expensive, what are your options for this to change? You can walk or cycle to work. You can cut back on spending in other areas of your life if you really do believe it is too expensive, as this is an essential in your everyday commute.

The complaining attitude that things in life are expensive is the reality created. Let's face it: everything in the world is going up in price. What are you going to do about it? Adapt to your basic needs. Do you need four cups of coffee per day? Why not go down to two or one and find a better way to keep yourself energised as opposed to purchasing several cups a day.

This is an attitude adjuster to reshaping your life. If the bus is something of an essential in your life, you need to audit your spending to find how this can be catered too. Will the bus then seem expensive to you? How does saying the bus is expensive add value to your life?

When you analyse your complaining or that of another, it highlights that there is nothing beneficial in doing so if you are not going to act on the situation. If you complained about a situation and you actually did something about it, that is a more productive way of attempting to change a situation and take control of your own emotional state.

To the one who complains and does nothing about it, you are literally pushing positive people away from you and drawing in the people who will resonate with you with in regards to the complaining state you are in. Do you want to be surrounded by people who complain all the time? I would certainly feel drained if there were no solutions offered.

This complaining I'm discussing here is not to be mixed up with facing true injustices. I am highlighting complaints with regards to everyday situations that are easily within our control.

Action Step: Your Attitude to Work

What is your attitude to work? Are you a person who hates Mondays? Where did this saying derive from? Why do people hate Mondays? The logical breakdown of this is weekends off and returning to work on Monday after a two-day break. I refuse to follow this mentality. I have shaped my attitude to work to be one where as much as I enjoy being off from work, I enjoy being at work too. As the leader of my workplace, my aim has been to create an environment where all team members feel they are fulfilling a purpose at work, thus making it a place to look forward to being.

Answer each question in the chart according to your situation.

Question	Self-Employed	Employee	Student
Why did I decide to …	create the business I have?	work where I am at present?	study my chosen course?
Why am I …	running this particular business?	still working here?	enjoying/not enjoying this course?
Am I happy …	when I'm working?	at work?	when I am studying?
If I am happy, what is it I …	love about my business?	love about my job?	love about my course?
If I am unhappy, what is it I dislike about …	my business?	my job?	my course?
Do I feel like I have a purpose …	when running my teams? (Or if working alone, do you feel your purpose?)	in my work team?	with my future direction?
If I do not feel like I have a purpose, what can I do to create my purpose?			

As mentioned previously, it is vital to take a step back in your life in any area you want to improve and analyse yourself. In jobs, we have to analyse situations. In social settings, we are conditioned to analyse how we interact with people. In public places, we analyse our surroundings. When do you actually analyse *you*?

In the example above, the setting has to do with a work environment. What we do for companies we work for is consistently analyse how we can make them better or do better. Within that, you can often lose your purpose of why you are doing the job you are doing in the first place. Putting yourself first is key. The above questions are all about you in your job role.

I will give an example of where I was as a department manager in a DIY store. This should assist you in relating to where you are currently.

1. *Why did I decide to work where I am at present?*

   Answer: To progress as a manager (whereas before I was a supervisor) and to work in a different company to show I can achieve in a different environment. I had been working in the same place for seven years, since I was a part-timer as a student.

2. *Why am I still working here?*

   Answer: I was working there to learn more about managing and how to influence sales. At the same time, it was a totally different team with a totally different personality set compared to where I was working before.

3. *Am I happy at work?*

   Answer: Honestly, at the time, I was not. The first few months were tough, and it had nothing to do with the job itself. It had to do with the bosses I was working for. It was a very aggressive culture, and I saw many managers crack under the pressure, breaking down in tears or walking out. I liked to think for myself and manage my time. We were expected to work twelve-hour shifts every day. If you left before twelve hours, that was frowned upon. This was the culture I was surrounded by, and it wasn't enjoyable. At the same time, the positive I was able to take away was the resilience of being able to tough it out there.

4. *If I am happy, what is it I love about my job?*
   Answer: During the happy times, I was happy with the team mentality I had with my colleagues, who ranged in age from 19 to 74 years old. The team had my back within my department. I also loved the engagement of the team with regards to their job role.

5. *If I am unhappy, what is it I dislike about my job?*
   Answer: As mentioned previously, it was the management culture of sacrificing personal time. Fortunately, I was just starting out in my career; therefore, I did not have huge commitments. I can imagine how it would have felt for a person with a family and not spending the quality time they wanted.

6. *Do I feel like I have a purpose in my work team?*
   Answer: In short, no. I felt more used for my skills as opposed to appreciation for them. There was a team that worked from eight to midnight daily to do the background work of the store, and we were on rotation for managing that between us department managers. I did run that shift very well; however, there came a point where my boss at the time wanted me to run that shift, and that was when I knew I was not growing in my job role and having a purpose to learn and grow.

7. *If I do not feel like I have a purpose, what can I do to create my purpose?*
   Answer: At the time, I created my purpose as getting things done. I built up a reputation for taking action and organising equipment, which benefited the whole store, not just my team. My team consisted of twenty people. The whole store team was around ninety, and it had an impact on them also. Yet I was not growing and developing to where I wanted to be. I felt ready to become an assistant manager as opposed to a department manager, so I decided to look elsewhere. I took on a job as an assistant manager in another company.

If I had to sum it up, I am very grateful for the experience I had with that particular DIY store. I learnt a lot about the high standards of the store and how to impact sales. I also learnt what not to do in terms of breaking your team's mental state.

My boss at the time wanted me to work six days—and remember, we were working twelve-hour days That would have been a seventy-two hour week had I worked six days. I came in as a favour for my boss at the time for a few hours on this sixth day, and he asked me where I was going when I left. I said, "I am going to the cinema with my friends."

He replied, "Whilst you are in the cinema watching the movie, I hope you will think about us watering your plants." (The garden section was also under my department). Aiming to lay guilt on your team is a trait some people use to rule by fear, as opposed to, "Well, enjoy your time off—well deserved."

I laughed off his comment and refused to absorb what he said. However, comments like that to other individuals could really bring them down. It is psychological manipulation, even if it is not intentional.

The point I am making here is I took the positives, and any negatives I experienced I was able to transmute by not treating my future teams in the same manner. The best advice I can give to those who are unhappy with their present situation is don't cry about it and don't give up. All you have to do is play the game temporarily and do things the way they want them done. Meanwhile, look elsewhere for a job that will give you more satisfaction. Never give up, as you are worth more than being influenced by external forces.

By taking this approach, you will reduce all the stress you have in your current environment. People will notice that extra spring in your step, as you know deep down you are creating change for yourself. This is how you grow and turn a negative situation into a positive.

If you do want to stay in your present job and feel you cannot look elsewhere, you must have the courage to voice your opinions on the environment created. Preparing bullet points (no pun intended) and raising these points with your boss is the best way to present your feelings in a purely factual manner. If you do have to escalate it further in the future, you will have on record that you raised this with your boss. Stay in your power always. No need to feel reactive/emotional.

When I was leading my own store, I found that my purpose became developing every single member of my team. I focused on bringing up the confidence levels of each individual. That was the purpose I created for myself, which led me into life coaching. Anyone can find a bigger purpose for the role they are doing.

Now relate those questions to yourself. Be brutally honest about how you feel. If you are enjoying your current role, this will assist you in coming up with an idea of how you can make a greater impact in your job role or work your way towards a promotion/extra responsibilities.

Value yourself enough to enjoy your work environment and take this step back. The action steps above will highlight your attitude towards your work and, more importantly, the self-analysis will assist in making you aware of what your attitude is in general. How you do anything is how you do everything.

Shining Your Light

Shining your light at work means transforming your attitude towards your job role, colleagues, and clients/customers. What is it you say about your boss? How do you describe your clients? How do you interact with your colleagues? All this has an impact on your attitude. The same goes for education. How you view your teachers/lecturers and your fellow students has an impact on your attitude.

For those who are football fans, this will be easy to relate to. Ole Gunnar Solskjaer, the manager of Manchester United, has taken over for a few months. In that time, he has brought the belief back to a club that had been struggling ever since Sir Alex Ferguson retired as the manager. The attitude Ole brought to the club that was missing since Sir Alex's time was the belief in the players and the belief to *win*, not just with the players but the staff of the club and the supporters.

The key thought I took away from this was from the pundit Rio Ferdinand, who said that Ole did not mention once in his prematch interview that Manchester United had ten injured players. No matter the circumstances with the team, Ole led with positivity, directness, and the belief to win.

We also apply these same winning attitudes in our job role or student life. No matter the odds, our attitude in coping with our environment is key to winning. This mentality, I promise you, gets picked up by everyone around you. That is how you shine your light.

When you implement this yourself in your own area, just notice how eventually, over time, everyone around you will pick this up. Stay in your power when you go for this, as you may come up against criticism or a put-down from a colleague or friend; it will feel uncomfortable to them that you have changed your mindset. Remember, it is comfortable for some people to be miserable or negative and complaining. If you begin to enjoy what you do, the people around you may want to bring you back down to keep themselves comfortable. But over time—or sometimes instantly—your light will spread. Become the golden bullet and move in one direction, which is forward.

CHAPTER 5

Shining Your Light in Your Personal Life

Achieving is not just about our work lives. How do you carry this energy of shining your light everywhere you go? What I have just mentioned above with regards to everyone picking up on this energy at work is true for your personal life too. That is where the inner work really transforms us—and this is where it gets really uncomfortable, but in a good way.

The one person you can be honest with is yourself. You must be alone to do this, as you will dissect why you behave the way you do. When you are analysing yourself by writing down on paper the personality traits you wish to change, this will highlight your current state. The interesting part will be how you are going to implement the desired changes.

In the previous chapter, we talked about confidence-building. Everything from realising your value within and being able to make decisions for yourself to analysing your own present state are all steps to building confidence without realising you are doing it. Confidence is not actively encouraged in schools and, funny enough, home life. If parents are not confident themselves, will the child pick up on this? Sometimes it happens.

To emphasise the point again: Confidence is not about being loud and overly expressive. Any personality type can be confident by communicating without hesitancy about what they accept or reject. Being able to say *no* to situations as well as *yes* takes confidence.

Yes-people who are always looking to please others and not themselves will one day realise they have not been true to themselves. Those who always says *no* to potential opportunities will one day realise they have not been true to themselves, as they have not lived by rejecting so many opportunities.

Pushing yourself out of your comfort zone should become second nature to you. If you do feel that rush in your stomach of excitement or anxious feelings, you must use that as a signal that this is a barrier you are going to break through. Otherwise, what will happen if you avoid these feelings? They will just come back again and again—until, of course, you bite your bullet.

There are people I know who have avoided situations or feelings from their past, and those feelings later crept up out of nowhere in their adult life. One person I know went past the age of 35 and then began having panic attacks one day. It was repressed feelings that had not been fully expressed catching up with this individual.

For those of you who are shy or nervous: No one feels sorry for you. They pity you that you are not living your best life. This is not cute shyness I am talking about; this is the shyness to put yourself out there with confidence that you can do something big. People can take advantage of you because they know you will not be speaking up or challenging back. The greatest news is that anyone can turn it around. No matter how much you think and believe you are not able to be that confident person, you can be.

The bullet that will follow you around forever until you bite it and crush it is the one that will not let you live to your full potential. Remember, your true self is the one that is able to express itself fully. It is how you communicate with the outside world that will define your confidence. Whether you are confident or feel you are not confident, go ahead with the following action step.

Action Step: Self-Analysis

Write your answers to the following down on paper.

- **Which area of your life do you want to build your confidence in?**
  Some examples of this are public speaking, approaching a potential partner, trying something new, pursuing the passion you have put off for a long time, going out more, travelling more, dressing to impress. Think about it deeply and honestly; perhaps there are other situations you are aware of that have been holding you back.

- **What do you *not* like about yourself?**
  This has been purposely worded to hit a message home. If you love everything about yourself, that is great. Ask yourself, *What would I like to improve about myself?* If the initial question hit home to you, go with it and really be brutal on yourself this one time. This could be the bullet spinning in front of you that you have not identified and faced. Once you have identified one or more traits that you feel are holding you back or that you wish to improve upon, move on to the next question.

- **How does this make you feel?**
  Why are we going through how it makes us feel? Because we are aiming to get really brutal on ourselves and expose the pain of why it is making us feel this way. If you begin tearing up about it or getting angry about it or any form of emotional response, then let that out. Really embrace this feeling, as it has been hiding for so long.

  List the feelings you have felt from this. Be really detailed with your feelings. If it has made you feel inadequate, sad, or lost, then really get deep into that. If you want to, write down how this has impacted your daily life and what thoughts come up because of it.

- **What past opportunities have been blocked because of this?**
  If there have been opportunities you have said no to or situations you have avoided, list these. You may have forgotten about these because you have been so used to feeling this way and having these thoughts about yourself that you are not aware of what you have pushed away.

An important note regarding this action step: When confronting feelings that you've buried for so long, it can take a few more confrontations to really get rid of it. The first time may be intense, and the second time may be even more intense. Or it could be less intense; it all depends on the individual. The point is, don't stop at the first sign of discomfort.

The first moment you experience of confronting these emotions is great. One week later, do it again to measure how you are feeling about it. If you remain committed to yourself on identifying and clearing these past moments, you will 100 per cent get there. The worst thing ever—which a lot of people go through in life—is to live with it for so long not realising that its always lingering in the background of your life. It is the bullet following you around everywhere.

I have seen people feeling great after confronting emotions over a breakup. They seem fine. When they confronted it again three weeks later, it was more intense than they had ever felt. Did they go in reverse? The easy thing for these individuals to feel at the time is that they have gone backwards, but this is far from the case. They are going even deeper within to rip out the pain. Keep going and continue. I promise you, it will fade over time more quickly when you confront it regularly with a small gap in between. You can do it.

Below are examples of how you might answer the questions above. The two topics chosen are ones that I have encountered over the years. I've included an analysis on each of these, as it could help you or someone you know in terms of their outlook on life. The examples use two common areas I have had feedback about from a number of types and ages of people. When I have had one-to-one sessions, these are the common answers that came up.

- **Which area of your life do you want to build your confidence in?**
    - nervous about speaking up
    - body image

- **What do you *not* like about yourself?**
    - I don't like that I am not able to voice my opinion.
    - The belly fat I have, I never used to.

- **How does this make you feel?**
    - Nervousness makes me feel disjointed from the groups I am in. I feel powerless that I am unable to speak up.
    - Belly fat makes me feel unattractive. I feel like giving up, so I continue to eat more junk. This becomes an endless cycle and has been more prominent in appearance as the years have gone and my belly has got bigger.

List the feelings you have felt from this.

- I feel shyness and timidity that I am unable to speak up. When people close to me have noticed this and have highlighted this as part of my personality, it makes me play that role by further reenforcing their impression of me as the quiet, shy person. I feel like I gave away my power.
- My body image makes me feel stuck and fed up that I am not doing anything about this. I feel inadequate that I cannot change it.

- **What past opportunities have been blocked because of this?**
    - Shyness: not being able to connect with others and make new friends/networks; passing the opportunity to say hello to a stranger who could have turned into a lover
    - Body image: No opportunities were missed. I had created that all in my head. I probably stopped myself from going swimming, as I didn't feel comfortable in exposing my belly.

The last question is worth highlighting. The shyness response regarding missing opportunities to connect with others is something that for some reason doesn't seem to matter at the time, but in reality, these individuals *did* want to connect with others in some form. They had pretty much talked themselves out of it before interacting with another person or a group in order to save embarrassment or effort.

It might not be that these shy individuals wanted to make lifelong friends, but imagine a situation at a party where you have mingled with various people. It may just be that shy people have felt left out because they were unable to show the world who they really are. Everyone was there to enjoy themselves, but when it came down to interacting with new, different people, they didn't show who they really were. It didn't have to be a performance, simply getting to know each other. Instead of putting themselves out there and living in the moment, they had many thoughts running through their head which prevented them from mingling.

The last question can really show you that it's a lot of what has been created in our own heads through overthinking a situation that in reality it isn't even so bad. We have made it more important than it really is.

The other answer regarding body image is important for everyone in terms of how we perceive ourselves. No one is going to care how we look as much as we do. If you own how you look, you don't have to be a body-builder or a swimsuit model to be and feel attractive. The attractiveness will come from the self-confidence you are learning to build and accepting who you are. Living a healthy lifestyle is different from wanting to look like a model.

How did you answer with your own list? Did the last question highlight any opportunities you missed, or was it more that you have been overthinking possible missed opportunities? Now that you have identified what it is about you that you have created in your mind, how do you feel? Do you feel like you can change, or are you still imagining you cannot? If you really want to master confidence, keep revisiting this list every week and rewriting your answers. Analyse how you have been throughout the week after reading this chapter and take an audit of how you are answering the questions above.

Whoever you are in terms of how much confidence you have, if there is any hardship you have been through, give yourself that quality time to look for whatever it is you have to clear from your past or an insecure feeling that creeps up now and again. This exercise is the most important action everyone should take for themselves. This should be taught in our schools so people are better equipped in adult life to confront these situations should they ever arise.

Doing this on your own is a very strong confidence-builder. When you look back on how you have identified and achieved this on your own, it can be uncomfortable to be forced to confront yourself or situations you have been through. That is why self-healing is important—so we can move forward, one step at a time.

Refrain from comparing your progress to others or to what your progress should be. Remember, the tree bears the fruit last. It is a journey for the apple. It does not appear in a second. Same goes for your confidence. Be patient with yourself and always remind yourself it is possible to become confident through dissecting each belief you have about yourself.

Forgiveness

Remember that the whole process of *Bite Your Bullet* is about you and you only. You are first in this and no one else. The past is dead weight that serves no purpose in your current reality and for the future reality you are creating. All it does is make you hold a grudge.

If there is a situation from the past or one person who has wronged you, how are you going to regain your power? The only way this is possible is through forgiveness and making peace with it in your own mind. The thoughts that can rise up through hanging out in previous situations are ones that continually creep up. This can happen in your sleep, when you are having a shower, when you are walking down the street—anytime, they can haunt you.

Yet it is very easy to stop them. I say with confidence that it is easy to put demons to rest. When you constantly confront these, you are able to lessen their power. The more you strive towards your goals, the less important the past becomes. By creating a new reality for yourself, you distance yourself from past mistakes or past pain.

What we'll cover in the next action step is forgiving yourself. It's not always an external factor that needs forgiving. Sometimes it's ourselves we need to forgive. We are so hard on ourselves that we stop ourselves moving forward because we can sometimes feel we don't deserve to. Again, that is something we have created ourselves and not necessarily true. Self-forgiveness is the highest love we can show ourselves.

Action Step 2: Forgiveness

Technique 1: Love the Thought

Loving the thought is something very powerful that I have discovered, and it is somewhat of a contradiction. If a thought comes up about a situation from your past—a regret, an ex, a failure, anything—you just have to love the thought. What I mean by this is, if any thought comes up in your head, no matter how bad it may appear to be, you have to say to yourself, "I love that." For example, you could be replaying a thought in your head about a past situation or person or an imaginary one. You have to say to yourself, *I love that thought*. By stating you love the thought, you confirm that it is the thought that exists, not the actual or made-up event.

You have to try this for yourself to feel it. You may even smile after doing it, as you feel a power overcome you. When you love the thought, automatically, as if by magic, the thought is no longer powerful. You own it. You immediately feel a sense of independence and freedom, as it no longer haunts your mind.

If the thought comes up again, love it again. Keep doing this until it means nothing. I assure you, if done correctly, with positive feeling and like you really mean it, then the thought will disappear. Smile as you love that thought. If you begin to feel uncomfortable or cry or something like that, you have a chance to overcome this barrier. It is a step towards forgiveness, but more importantly, freedom.

I discovered this technique through my own experience. One night, I could not get to sleep at all. I was thinking of an ex-girlfriend and things that had gone wrong in the past. I couldn't shake it off. I was alone in my room and it was pitch black, as I was trying to sleep. Constantly thinking about this ex got me even more worked up. Trying to forget the thoughts was not helping either. This lasted four hours, and I was all the while aware that I had to get to sleep and wake up for work the next morning.

How could I get out of this cycle? Where would the breakthrough come? I had no idea, and I had no intention of breaking the cycle I was literally stuck in with these thoughts about the ex and how certain things happened in the relationship. These thoughts were wasted energy. I had no control of the past, yet I could not stop thinking about it. I refused to go on my phone, as I did not want to distract myself meaninglessly for the sake of occupying my mind. Avoiding the situation was no good at all.

All of a sudden, four hours later, I have no idea how it happened, but I began to love the thought—a powerful form of accepting the thought. When you love the thought as opposed to accepting it, you rise above acceptance. Read that back again for it to make sense and so you can absorb it. Say you think of something bad, such as crashing your car. These random thoughts can pop up for no reason. When you love the fact that you can crash, the thought disappears. When we have bad thoughts we do not want, we usually attempt to avoid them out of fear. The more we do this, the more we think about them, as it creates a *What if this happens?* scenario.

What I am highlighting here is something that is hardly spoken about: loving a thought. Think of it as a double negative. In maths, when you have a double negative, it automatically becomes a positive: $-2 \times -2 = +4$. It is exactly the same with thoughts. Loving a negative thought does not make sense, but the outcome you have is one of freedom.

What happened to me that night was that I became liberated from my thoughts. I gained full power over them. Identifying the pain and spitting out the pain from the past all play a part, but the final part of loving the thought is something that truly liberates you.

People I have life-coached to love the thought have found it successful too. I had one client who had negative thoughts about a past decision she made when she was a teenager. It left her feeling guilty every time she was alone with her thoughts. At the time, when she was a teenager, it seemed right. Analysing the situation today, it was the right thing to do. She has excelled so much in her personal life, has a family, and is doing well.

To respect the identity of this particular client, I am unable to go into the details of her situation. However, this particular lady loved the thought of feeling guilty. The feedback I received from her was that she felt really light and free. She then went on to describe in detail that, when she was alone, she felt no anxiety or regret for the first time in fifteen years.

The change in those I have coached in this technique has been excellent. They're achieving their life goals and working towards what they want to do. I am grateful to have played a part in their life and their ability to feel good again.

I explained this process to my best friend the day after it came to me, and he put it into better words for me, as he assisted in making us both understand how this works. His take on it was that loving the thought ultimately gives you power over the thought, and you feel above that level of thinking. As a result, that thought has no power over you.

With my own experience at the time, when I loved the thought of my ex and I no longer being together, it immediately brought a smile to my face, and the tension I felt vanished. It happened as if by magic. I cannot explain it, but it is definitely a technique I wish everyone would use. I am sure any emotions you have will begin to follow a new positive direction and liberate your mind.

Technique 2: Forgive Yourself

The second technique is about forgiveness: forgiving others and then forgiving yourself. Forgive yourself for holding on to something so long it has halted your progress. The quicker you forgive, the quicker you can move forward.

Write the following paragraphs down, filling in the blank line with a person's name or an event that you *need* to forgive.

- **Forgiving others/or outside situations**
  I am ready to forgive _____, as I know they have acted from a place of fear within themselves or desperation to control me. It shows their weakness. I wish them the best and forgive them—not for them, but for me. I am important, and I deserve to be free. I am free.

- Forgiving yourself
  I am ready to forgive myself, as I deserve the best for myself. I have forgiven others, and I am at peace with them. I now have to be at peace with myself, and I forgive myself for _____. By forgiving myself, I am now able to continue forward with my life, appreciate everything about myself, and share my best self with the world.

Spitting Out the Pain

Spitting out the pain and clearing the past is a journey we all must take. We hear of people who are traumatised by situations that happened to them in their early childhood or as an adult. Some are never the same again, and the person they once were has vanished and been lost.

Some of us carry guilt with us for many years. One day, when we want to do something about our current state of life, we forget who we are or what time we have wasted on thoughts that were imaginary and make us feel like we have carried a large boulder around weighing us down. As teenagers, we may be reckless and feel we will never regret anything—until one day, when we have become a little wiser, we begin to reflect on what has happened and where life has taken us. That is why forgiveness of others is for ourselves to be free, and forgiveness for ourselves is the ultimate forgiveness. This is the thing that holds us back the most in life, where we critic ourselves till we become hollow.

Fill yourself up now. The next part of building confidence is rebuilding ourselves. We are on the right track for becoming confident. Going through the clearing stage and confronting the pain is the first step.

CHAPTER 6

Boundary-Setting

After we have gone through the fire, so to speak, of clearing our past and current pain, now comes the fun part. I call it *fun* as it is exciting to rediscover who we are and what we intend to do with our future. Setting boundaries is another form of self-love. We are respecting our own time and space and allowing our time and energy to be where we want it to be. It is another boundary of how we want to be treated.

Why is this so important? Often, we may have found ourselves pleasing others, such as accepting invitations to places and events we do not want to attend. Sometimes these invitations we accept are an escape from our own procrastination. I'll hold my hand up high that when I was a student and had homework to do or coursework, I would say yes to going out with friends. That would have been my excuse for delaying completion of the work.

Saying yes to something we do not want to do or shouldn't do is one boundary crossed. Another is allowing others to disrespect us, whether through their words or their actions towards us. If we do not set boundaries and go along with other people's requests, we have taught them how we want to be treated.

On the flip side, if you have stated your boundary clearly to others, you have taught them how you wish to be treated. If you have said no to going to a party and you want to spend time crafting a business plan at home or doing weights at the gym, and your friends and sometimes family do not respect that part of you, then that is their problem, not yours. Truly believing in yourself means you know what you are doing—and, more importantly, why you are doing it.

This social aspect is one example. I am sure you have other areas of your life where you may have encountered this. Perhaps you had set yourself a goal of no alcohol for a month and you gave in to drinking alcohol with a peer group. The way you feel after is the worst, because you strayed from a goal you had initially set yourself.

This is not to be confused with becoming highly stubborn and rigid in your ways, where you only stick to your reality. Coming back to relationships with others always involves an element of compromise. The boundary-setting we are highlighting here has to do with how we feel in certain situations and putting our well-being first in order to recharge or make time for personal goals we wish to achieve.

The example mentioned earlier in this book regarding a relative of mine, Sigmund, who completed his university degree is a great example. He set his own boundaries in order to make time for something he found important. He knew this was a temporary project for himself, and he stuck to it. If his family members encouraged him to take a break from his studying or to go out somewhere, he stood by his boundary and focussed on what he is doing.

Healthy Boundaries

In relationships, how you wish to be treated should be set from the beginning or early stages. If there is a red flag early in the relationship, it's easy to ignore it and continue. What tends to happen is that further down the road, this becomes a bigger annoyance to you, and arguments can start. Remember, this is a sensitive area for your boundary. If you have established what your boundary is for you personally and you are entering a relationship, you have to stick to your level of self-respect, otherwise you end up giving too much of yourself to the other person, who can begin to take advantage of this. This works the other way, too—if you know your partner has not set boundaries, think of how you are behaving. Are you taking advantage of that person by overstepping personal boundaries?

You have no obligation to be the person of someone else's image. The aim of building solid confidence in ourselves is so we can be independent from the world and from other people's moods and energy. If someone doesn't want to be around you, then you have to be confident and secure enough in yourself that you realize that person has something going on. You can try to ask that person a question to provide assistance, but ultimately, that individual may need some space to figure it out.

In the journey of self-confidence, you may end up losing people around you. This is not a bad thing at all. A new version of you may not be what others are used to, as they have built up a familiar image of you based on how you have been throughout their life.

Moving Forward

One person I coached, who we'll name Nelson, had dreams of becoming a billionaire. He wanted to progress financially in his life. Nelson was jobless at the time. He had finished his education and came out with very good grades. He had a set of friends he'd grown up with who were not bad people.

One evening, Nelson and his group of friends were hanging out on a street outside of one of the friends' car. They were all dressed in hoodies and joggers and were perhaps quite loud in enjoying themselves. A police car pulled up beside them. The police were accusing them of having drugs on them and hinting towards them being up to no good. The reality is they, were just talking.

The part I highlighted to Nelson was that he was always there for his friends and highly available to them. In doing this, Nelson would neglect his goals. His goals of succeeding in becoming financially stable and then abundant were not moving forward because he was not committing to himself 100 per cent. His friends, who smoked drugs and were not as driven as Nelson, were happy living their life day to day, but that was not Nelson's goal.

The conclusion for Nelson was to move forward. If they were truly his friends, they would be happy for him, and they would not think anything differently of Nelson for committing to his goals. If you are in a similar position in terms of choosing your friends always over yourself, you have to make that same sort of decision and stick to it.

Another example, also a true story: A person I know, who we'll call Sean, told about one of his friends who became a multi-millionaire. We'll name the millionaire Doug. During the '80s, Sean and five of his friends would drink whiskey together every Friday. Doug was part of this group. He then began to drink less with them on Fridays. Eventually, Doug took up accounting jobs for his boss and would stay late completing these.

One of the friends from the group would begin taunting Doug and calling him names like kiss-ass for staying late all the time. He would swear at Doug too. Eventually, Doug began to not hang out with those friends anymore. Sean explained that this other friend would talk badly about Doug and how he was a sell-out.

Long story short: Doug is now a multi-millionaire with his own export company. The friend who would swear at Doug is still in the same profession as he was during the '80s. There is no right or wrong in terms of profession. But the idea that someone would belittle a friend for wanting to improve his life can be draining. Doug's story is a very good one, and one I highlighted to Nelson also, of how when you stay focussed on your goal and have boundaries set, you can achieve anything you want. Doug set his boundary and chose not to live that lifestyle of routinely drinking away every week.

Again, I repeat, there is no right or wrong in how anyone wishes to live life. But I take inspiration from Doug's way of living. He is proof that staying focussed and on track for where you want to be can get you there.

Time

Setting a boundary for your time is highly important for you own well-being and development. If you are too available to other people, when is there time for yourself?

Some of you may have felt drained by interacting with different sets of friends, family, or clients, and then you feel like you have done nothing for yourself. Putting others first is not a quality that is highly noble and will be rewarded somehow. The reality is that when looking after your own well-being first, you will give quality interaction that others will appreciate even more.

If someone has asked you for help in a particular situation, and that person is important to you but you are not feeling great yourself, how are you going to give your best advice or support to that person? It is about being honest and letting that person know you are not in the headspace you need to be. You will be with them as soon as you can. The following are some boundary settings to take into consideration.

Your Own Time

When you analyse how you have lived your life, you may well get to a point where you have not really done anything for yourself. People-pleasing is one example of your time being a boundary where you dedicate one hour per day to yourself, as a minimum. In that hour, you may wish to work out, read, listen to music, draw, or any of an endless number of options. You may have signed up to an online study course and keep telling yourself you have no time.

If you have extra responsibilities of being a carer or a parent, then yes, you may feel as if time escapes you. However, when you analyse each of these boundaries, you'll create the boundaries with your children too. Remember the TV show *Supernanny*? Boundaries can be created with your kids in terms of your time—in a tactful manner, of course, as we don't want to neglect them or make them feel unloved in any way.

Think back again to the airplane instructions. They always state that when the oxygen masks fall down from above, put one on yourself first and then administer it to your child. It is the same thing for everyday life. If you are creating a better understanding of yourself, you will be able to give quality interaction to your kids. If you are a leader in your field at work, the same applies. When you manage your own time, the quality of your mental state will be beneficial to the team you lead.

Your Own Space

A married woman once told me she sometimes takes a long route home to delay reaching home. It's not to avoid her husband but just to have a bit of me-time to unwind from her day. It is nothing personal against her husband. I also have a close friend who has informed his wife that he needs thirty minutes to himself when he gets home to switch off from his day, and then he spends quality time with her.

The communication aspect is very important, so you can understand each other's needs and wants. In the first example, the woman did not communicate this to her partner. It was something for her only. And I understand where she is coming from. Sometimes we don't want to explain anything to anyone and just do something for ourselves. In the second example, he used public transport, so I guess he had no cause for delaying his journey, yet he communicated he wanted some time to reset himself.

This doesn't just apply to couples or people in relationships. Single people can have a lot of people wanting their time. The best advice is to plan what you wish to do in that space of yours. Fill it with as much as you want. Sitting in front of the TV can be cool. However, are you guilty of channel-surfing or watching a repeat of a programme just for the sake of it being on in the background? Challenge yourself on what you really want to do in your own space.

Meditation or deep-breathing is something that can centre you from the chaotic day you have had or being in the warrior mode of achieving throughout your day, where you are constantly on edge. Try a social media timeout. Our smartphones and social media are part of our lives, both personal and business. The timeout is highly important for switching off the constant stimulus we get from social media.

Experiment with the social media groups that you are in. Put them on mute (there are settings where you can mute all groups without having to go through each one individually and for whatever duration you wish to mute them for). You'll find the individual messages you have received from others may not be so important. Keep your phone away from you for an hour, and you'll find you really don't need to be on your phone as much as you believe.

Take it a step further and dedicate a time you wish to look at your phone and set that boundary for yourself of when you wish to stop. If it's thirty minutes, then keep to that. The fear of missing out (FOMO) is what can halt our confidence, as we can create an insecurity where we have to be up to date.

Haven't got time for the gym? Haven't got time for hobbies? Haven't got time for a study course? Well, put your phone in check with your boundaries and see how much time you free up for yourself. You will feel liberated.

How You Wish to Be Treated by Others.

This is a big one for self-confidence-building and self-love in general. In any relationship you have with others, this is your world they are interacting with. Why should your boss, work colleague, friend, family member, or partner make you feel low? I mean consistently low, not just one-off arguments, even if they make you feel high. Why is how you feel dependant on them?

Once you have gone through all the steps in the previous chapters, you will come to know yourself even more. With knowing yourself comes a knowledge of how you would like to be treated through others' actions or words. You will not tolerate people disrespecting you through passive aggressive comments, aggressive behaviour, belittling you with comments, and sometimes attempting to embarrass you.

The cliché we were taught in school about talking to the person is exactly what you need to do. Don't be afraid to be a little madder than you usually are if you have been bottling it up for a long time. Keep it in check, though—please, nothing crazy.

Sometimes the people around us may unintentionally embarrass us in front of others without knowing how it can make us feel. A simple one-on-one conversation should straighten it out. Speaking calmly is the best way to approach it when you highlight the other person's action and what your perception of it was. If you want to describe how you felt and think it's beneficial, then by all means do it.

If it is your boss who is making you feel low, it's your turn to manage that individual. This is where you ask your boss to coach and develop you so you can see the boss's vision. This may highlight to the boss another way of working as opposed barking out instructions and expectations.

Self-confidence is all about expressing yourself in a secure manner. Obviously, we don't want to turn into snowflakes and be offended by everything everyone does. This is about those situations where you feel disrespected by something. Bottling it up is the worst thing you can do, as it affects your own mental well-being. This is what past generations have done, and it's time to break that cycle. Bottling up feelings will only cause you to make wrong decisions in other areas of your life. You may feel irritated with your kids, partner, or colleagues if you are bottling up feelings inside, because you are not able to communicate this.

If you are a leader in your field of work, I encourage you to spot the behaviours of your team as well. If there are people on your team who are generally quiet or seem timid, take the one-on-one time with them to open them up a bit more. Encourage them to feel like they are part of the team as opposed to isolating themselves. You may find they will work for you even better knowing they have built a rapport with you.

When you become confident as a leader, it is easy for the rest of the team not to speak up or challenge you. However, the true leader is one who uplifts others and makes them feel part of the team with input.

The way you know your team is engaged is through the input they are giving you. If you have not created a culture of the team being able to input, then that is something to work on.

The new era is all about the well-being of each individual. You will find that the more you start believing in yourself and developing self-confidence, the more you will find yourself around people who respect you for who you are. Referring back to leaders: even if you are working under someone else, you can still be a leader of positive change helping those around you feel good.

Away from the work world, we are all leaders—leaders of our life. Leaders who are confident around everyone in any environment inspire those around them. You will notice friends and family start communicating with you differently. The boundary-setting of how you wish to be treated is literally you coaching others on that topic and leading by example by treating them the same way.

If you have been that shy type and have never set the boundaries with anyone before, this is your chance to do so with the people you interact with on a daily basis, through coaching and developing. Leadership is basically coaching and developing. That is why anyone can become a leader. The only work you have to do is be consistent with it and not feel shy if you get knocked back. It's a perceived knock back if someone makes a comment towards you. Own your standard and watch how the relationships around you become more positive.

The Standard You Set for Yourself

Take stock of your own self. What boundaries have you created for yourself independent of others? What I mean by this is, what are you eating? What are you doing to take care of your health in general? What type of people do you wish to surround yourself with?

Why is this important? Surrounding yourself with forward thinkers and leaders gives you something you feel inspired by. It can be as simple as watching an inspirational talk online, such as Ted Talks, or the inspirational volunteer work you have seen people do. What standard are you feeding your mind now? This is the rebuilding phase of Project You. The standard you are setting yourself is one which meets your new reality.

If you want to go to sleep at ten every night, that is a standard you are setting for yourself. Your *why* may be that it improves your quality of sleep and your overall mood when you wake up.

Owning your standard means you are being a leader to everyone around you and creating the standard. This is by no means forcing people to act a certain way. This is literally you creating a win-win scenario for all involved. Think of win-win scenarios in your social circles and imagine how you can influence this.

When You Wake Up, Get Up

This one is highly important and one that can take real willpower to get you through. I remember waking up when I was a kid. I would want to get out of bed as soon as possible, full of energy to attack the day. Then came the teenage years, where I would want to lay in after I opened my eyes. Back then, there was no social media to keep you distracted. There was only the TV to keep on and just stay in bed. This is not a bad thing to do, nor is being on your smartphone as soon as you wake up.

However, try the following for yourself and see how you feel: As soon as you wake up, get up out of bed. If you are older and not in great health, then get up slowly. Sit up first in your bed and then stand up. If you are fit and healthy, then as soon as you open your eyes, get out of bed.

The classic pressing of the snooze button for the extra ten minutes only makes us feel like we are dragging our day forward instead of feeling well rested. If you have trouble waking up, you need to get to the root of your sleeping pattern. If you can commit to yourself to getting out of bed as soon as you open your eyes and then making your bed straight away, you are already starting your day in a winning mentality. Of course, it can take time to adjust to this for some us who have been used to laying in for a long time, but the benefit you will feel is one of success and optimism for the day ahead.

This is especially true for anyone going through depression—when you wake up, you feel there is no point in getting up. But I have to encourage you to take that step and keep repeating it daily. Look at the tips below on how you can train yourself to wake up and get up.

Why have I placed this as a boundary? Well, you can easily set yourself boundaries for waking up. It may be that in the beginning, you say to yourself, "I will not stay awake in bed for more than ten minutes." And as each day passes, you may attempt to decrease it by one minute. The ultimate goal is getting out of bed within ten seconds, not reaching for your phone or anything. You come first, not your phone or anyone else.

Whilst on this topic: This is not to go against the occasional days where a lay-in is wanted—not needed, but wanted. This is for the readers who really want to develop their goal-oriented mind and take a step in building confidence.

I encourage a thirty-day challenge for this. See how you feel. I am confident that when getting yourself out of bed in this way, you'll notice a difference in your mental well-being. The bullets we create for ourselves come from not knowing what to do with the extra time we have. By getting out of bed and cracking on with our day, we begin to find this extra time.

In that extra time, you can do the meditation or deep-breathing you wish to do in the beginning of the day. You can set your intentions by compiling a list. Better yet, you can eat a proper breakfast. You'll be surprised in a pleasant way by the happiness you have found in doing this, as your general mood feels much better.

The Physical Environment You Create for Yourself

This goes in sync with the above. It is a culmination of everything mentioned regarding how you want to create your physical surroundings. Have a look at your own time and space, whether it be your room, study area, or workspace. Is it clear and organised for your use? A messy environment can be quite noisy for the mind.

If you have a non-spiritual outlook on life, the science itself states clutter can affect anxiety if you are constantly exposed to it. It can even depress you if you are surrounded by it all the time. If you are spiritual, there is feng shui, where clutter is classed as negative energy. You don't even need to be a scientist or a spiritualist to know how you feel when environments are clean and organised, and how you feel when they are cluttered and messy.

Conclusion

How does boundary-setting link to confidence? Everything about it links to confidence-building. You are taking control of your life by doing this whole rebuilding stage. These steps can transform your life. I encourage readers to read the above as much as you feel you need to in order for this to settle into your mind and be put into practice.

Boundary-setting means being strong enough to communicate to others who you really are. There is nothing fake about it. You know yourself and what standard you are attempting to set. These are tools for developing shy people into confident people who believe in themselves. The techniques may seem like they do not connect to confidence, but a quick breakdown will display how the process works.

Boundaries regarding *time* and *space* build your confidence as a means of knowing what you want to do in your own time and space. Knowing you *have* a time and space is self-assuring, and you are not going to let this control you.

Boundaries regarding *how you wish to be treated* and *the standard you set yourself* build confidence because you know what you want in life through your interactions with others and at the same time inspire those around you by the way you conduct yourself.

Boundaries regarding *when you wake up and get up* and *your physical environment* build confidence because getting up as soon as you can is a kind of confidence in itself. You are training yourself mentally that you are ready for the day ahead. Making up your bed and your physical environment is a win in itself too. You will be returning home to a made-up bed and not a messy one. It all links together.

CHAPTER 7

Assured Body Language and More Confidence-Builders

We are now on the right track for becoming confident. The first step was going through the clearing stage and confronting the pain. The second step was boundary-setting, which is the rebuilding stage. Now we turn to transforming our body language.

Body language is a form of communication. When you see a person who may feel down about something, you can see their shoulders hunched over or their neck drooping downward whilst they stare at the floor. Facial expressions are a giveaway too. You can tell if someone is anxious or worried about something. Usually, when people are highly nervous, you can see them fidgeting, as they are uneasy about something.

If soldiers in the army were allowed to stand any way they wished to, what would that communicate to us all? Imagine a soldier slouching and holding a weapon casually. You would not view that individual as threatening or assured. You would lose faith that such a soldier could protect you. The queen's guards are the same; if you saw them outside Buckingham Palace and they were not standing upright, you would not see them as having authority or presence.

I look at my own journey of body language from when I was in high school. I remember, for whatever reason, that to protect myself and show I was strong to the rest of my friends in high school, I would automatically stand up straight with my chin up. At the time, it was my priority in my social circles that I wanted to be the strong one. It actually gave me a psychological edge over the others in sports. I was not of a large frame, but I had that confidence in myself.

Fast-forward to when I was a weekend supervisor in my retail job whilst I was at uni. I went through a bit of a rough patch by having drama with a girl I dated. When I was at work, I remember being quite tense. The new store manager at the time—who you may remember was Pearl—was very fiery when she first joined as the new leader of the department store I worked in. Pearl noticed my hunched-over body language and commented, "How do you think your team views you? You have no presence. You don't even stand up straight!"

I was going through a rough time back then at age 21, and reflecting back on it, I didn't realise that it affected my body language. These things you cannot hide if you are not feeling great and confident. It was a good reminder for me, though, when Pearl pointed this out.

I became conscious of my body language again. Once I had gotten through the drama with that particular girl at the time, I was well on my way to being myself again. My body language was back to how I was before. I would be walking around the store with a straight back and head up. When I spoke with customers, they had more trust in me. When speaking with my colleagues, some of them commented that I would walk around with authority. This was not my goal. I was simply focussed on the goals I had to achieve with the team, and this must have given them further trust that I was leading them.

There are many videos on YouTube about confident body language. It is important to communicate this to everyone else to build that trust and rapport through non-verbal communication. Whether you are at work or in your personal space with social circles, always carry that stature by appearing alert and ready. By standing up straight and sitting up straight, naturally you will feel more confident just in that moment.

Action Step: Body Language Confidence

Before doing the following, I would encourage you to record yourself. Seeing yourself and how you are with non-verbal communication is a real eye-opener. We never get to analyse our physical selves from an external point of view unless we have seen ourselves on a short video clip. This is the task of you communicating through to yourself basically like a silent movie actor. Follow these steps to enact non-confident body language:

1. Sit alone with no distractions
2. Sit on a chair or the edge of your bed—anywhere you can sit properly.
3. Slouch forward as how you think a non-confident, shy, timid person would sit.
4. Begin fidgeting with your hands as if you are nervous.

How did you feel? If you recorded yourself, play it back and make notes on what your interpretation is of yourself from an outside view. How do you feel after seeing yourself back?

Purposely acting like a non-confident person should trigger something inside you and remind you how powerful this really is—communicating to other people when we may not mean to be like this. The feeling you have felt from behaving like that should make you not want to revisit that feeling ever again. Seeing yourself that way if you recorded yourself may make you cringe. Remember that feeling and know that it is not how you are going to be.

Now follow these steps to enact confident body language:

1. Sit alone with no distractions.
2. Sit on a chair or the edge of your bed—anywhere you can sit properly.
3. Sit upright with a very straight back. Hold your head up, with your chin almost raised to a 45 degree angle. Keep your shoulders relaxed and slightly back.
4. Sit like this for a minute. Practice slow movements. Maybe keep a pen on the table. What are you going to be doing with the pen? Are you going to be fidgeting with it? No: slow movements. Pick up the pen fairly calmly and slowly. Turn your head in different

directions in the way you feel calm and confident people would move their head. Whilst you are seated like this, be aware if you are fidgeting with your feet or anything like that. Visualise yourself as a strong, large mountain that is filling up the space around you.

How did you feel? If you recorded yourself, can you see the difference? More importantly, how do you feel seeing a very confident version of yourself? What are you seeing that is communicated when you behave like that?

Have more fun with the above examples, if you like. You may want to imagine yourself in a coffee shop, a meeting room, anywhere you want. But the main point of this is to act as you believe you should be when you are confident. That cringing feeling of seeing yourself as not confident is very effective in making you want to change your ways.

Next, you can try the same recording of yourself but walking. Notice how you are walking. If you are walking too fast, do you look nervous? If you are walking calmly, do you feel assured? When you are out and about in public next time, be conscious of how you are walking. Make the adjustment of walking upright.

The biggest contest we face in body language is with our smartphones. Consistently we are forced to look down at our phones. If you look at our neck, we are forcing it to look down a majority of the time. Subconsciously, we get used to this. Use this time to make yourself aware of how you are holding and carrying yourself.

Being aware of how you are carrying yourself will keep you on the right path of feeling confident through your body. Whether you are male or female, this confident body language conveys trust and assurance. It's important to note that you are not doing this for others. This is for yourself. Another bonus of having good posture is that it will keep your body strong into old age and prevent too much slouching.

Feel the confidence flow through you when you are seated upright. Practice sitting like this as much as you can until it becomes a habit. When you have been seated for quite some time, make a self-observation as to whether you have slouched over without realizing it.

Can you feel the difference in yourself when you sit upright? Do you feel powerful and invincible just sitting upright in a calm and collected manner? You should be feeling more in control of yourself and ready for anything. When you are in any form of meeting, remember to sit like this, and you'll notice how alert you feel.

We are on the right track for becoming confident:

Step 1—Going through the clearing stage and confronting the pain
Step 2—Boundary-setting, which is the rebuilding stage
Step 3—Assured body language

We will now move on to step 4: try something new.

Learning a New Skill or Doing Something New

True confidence allows you to be yourself anyplace and anytime. We are speaking of personality here, not skills. I am not expecting everyone to become confident in mastering a new skill overnight, such as learning a new sport/language or driving a car. But approach that new skill with confidence, and you will be able to pick it up more efficiently.

The benefits of learning something new also have a scientific element within our brains. New neural pathways are created. This feeling of learning a new skill becomes reenforced the more we practice it. As you revisit the new task or activity, you'll find that you are feeling more. confident that you are progressing.

Imagine learning something new every few weeks. Think of the skill set you would be building for yourself. Think of how passionately you would be able to talk to someone else about what you are doing. In turn, you'll inspire others to act on learning something new.

Put yourself out there and join a class if you have to. Over time, you'll not only build your confidence in learning but also create new networks with people you meet. Let this all unfold naturally. Don't try to force any new connections or force your learning. Be so engrossed in your learning that everything else that happens around it is a by-product.

If you meet some new people, great! If you feel more confident as you learn, great! Practice makes perfect, right?

As you have taken the steps to do your clearing and present yourself to the world through your body language, now it's time to fill yourself up with these new skills. When shy personality types learn a new skill, they often give up at the first sign of a perceived failure. But once they are able to express themselves more freely because their confidence has grown, learning is accelerated. They enjoy what they are doing and are less self-conscious.

When you are learning something new and not enjoying it, your progress can seem slow. At times, you may feel like giving up. However, when you improve your ability to express yourself, you are freer to enjoy learning and attempting new things, as you are out of your thoughts (imaginary bullets) and more into the present moment.

Remember to carry that body language with you when you are in a new environment of learning. From the beginning, your teachers/mentors will want to involve you more, as they see that you are taking the class seriously. They will bounce off your energy and want you to succeed. This comes back to the win-win scenario.

There are thousands of activities or courses to help you learn something new, including boxing, running, gym, painting, singing, dancing, or a home study course. Everyone has that passion inside ready to be pursued. You may have been reluctant to do so because of what others will think. But this step forward in confidence is the decision you make.

You have done the clearing, and that should already have pumped you up that you are personally overcoming this situation. You have set your boundaries, which should further inspire you that you are recognising your true character and values. You are carrying yourself like a champion, and now you have that winning feeling in your step. You are ready. Do something new.

Consider your routines. They can become mundane. You want to break out of the cycle. Friends who have been socialising on a set day want to break out of that routine, as they want to use that time to do something else. People who wake up every morning at seven want to have more time for breakfast, so they might do something new and wake up at six fifteen. These breaks and jolts to our routines can be confidence-boosting.

You don't have to go telling the whole world or announcing to the world over social media that you are making these changes for yourself. The quiet confidence in yourself you will be creating is more than enough to give you fuel to make it through your day.

Action Step: Affirmation

Make up your own affirmation that you can look at daily. Write it down on a note card and look at it multiple times throughout the day. Say it out loud. If you drive on your way to work, say it out loud. If you don't drive, find a space to say it to yourself quietly.

The following are some examples of affirmations:

- "I am the most confident, strong, powerful person I can be in all areas of my life, and I am loving it."
- "I know I am confident, and I love this feeling."
- "My confidence inspires everyone around me."

Use one of these or make up your own. Make them as short or long as you want. These are your truths you are speaking about.

Are We Confident Yet? We Are Confident!

When we are truly confident, there is no need to ask a question whether we are or not. Refrain from measuring yourself by your level of confidence. It is always evolving and strengthening, like a muscle. Keep telling yourself you are confident.

We have now made it through five steps:

Step 1—Going through the clearing stage and confronting the pain
Step 2—Boundary-setting, which is the rebuilding stage

Step 3—Assured body language
Step 4—Learning something new or doing something new
Step 5—Creating your affirmation and using them to reshape your thinking.

Action Step: Keeping a Log

As a final action step for confidence-building, keep a log of all the steps above. You'll be able to see how far you have come in your journey. The beginning tasks may have left you feeling low on confidence. Revisit those to remind yourself of how far you have come or as a reminder of what areas you still need to work on. Review everything you have done. I encourage you to keep a file with all the action steps as a reminder of the investment you have put into yourself.

Bonus Level: Confidence from Self-Defence and Standing Up for Yourself

This topic is slightly controversial, as it involves violence. Before I continue, let me say that I am by no means endorsing violent behaviour or abuse of others with physical force. There can be attackers carrying weapons, such as knives or even guns, and I am not suggesting that anyone should be foolhardy and jump towards someone carrying a weapon. Nor do I mean you should go out into dangerous territory to confront this situation.

The reason for incorporating physical power is the strengthening of inner confidence. When you know the limits of how you can fight, there is a new level of confidence you experience within, and it branches out into all areas of your life. Again, this is not an excuse to walk around arrogant and cocky, where you are pissing people off by being a show-off. Think of Mr Myagi in the movie *The Karate Kid*. He could kick anyone's ass, but he did not go around boasting about it. He remained centred and respectful and fought only when he was attacked or saw others getting attacked.

The kind of confidence I am highlighting is where you avoid becoming numb when confronted by a dangerous person. They are used to behaving in a low-mannered way, where they wish to intimidate and inflict pain on another human. We all need to have the confidence to stand up to the behaviour, shouting at them to make others aware. The whole point of the previous confidence steps is to be able prevent an attacker from even considering approaching you, as you are projecting confidence and do not appear vulnerable. That is because you genuinely are not vulnerable with those behaviours.

The point of bringing this topic up is that when you are confronted with a dangerous scenario, there is a different kind of confidence required to defend yourself and strike at someone who is attempting to attack you or attack other innocent people. Where police or security are not on hand and it is only yourself and an attacker left, what are you meant to do? The whole point of self-defence is to not ever have to use it.

Ideally, you would diffuse situations through verbal communication. However, I live in reality, and when I have seen presenters on TV addressing violent behaviour in the streets, they are disconnected from how the street mentality can work and believe that educating offenders will deter them. When muggers want to mug you, they have no moral compass for their actions. If they attempt to snatch your bag, what are you going to do? Their mission is to steal and potentially harm.

Here are scenarios where physical violence can occur and where self-defence is required:

- a mugging
- attempted rape
- a bully becoming physical
- seeing an innocent person attacked where you will have to intervene

If someone larger than you grabs you, how are you going to react? I have seen people become numb and not say anything. The aggression in the attacker's face is a scary sight for the person being attacked. The fear the victim feels is energy for the attacker.

In these situations where an attack is taking place, projecting your voice and a never-say-die attitude is what is required. You need to have balls of steel and become a warrior. Ladies, you have to be a bad bitch and turn nasty. I am not saying to punch the attackers, as they can be stronger than you. You have to have the confidence to shout in their face, "No!" Then strike them in the face if possible and run for help.

You have to make a lot of noise. People who lack confidence would not make too much noise. This is the time where your boundary is being crossed, and you have to protect yourself by any means necessary and alert others of danger. If the offenders try to tell you to shut up or be quiet, you can rattle them with your confidence and alert everyone you can.

Become comfortable with striking. Where you have access to a punchbag, definitely use it and practice daily if possible. The idea is that if you have never encountered violence growing up, you must know what it feels like to strike at something. Even better is to enrol in self-defence classes.

Boxing clubs I have found to be really beneficial. When sparring, you really can get hit, and so you lose any fear of getting hit, as you now know what it feels like. Grappling sports such as MMA/Judo are really good too, where it is close combat and it gets a bit rough. Karate, aikido, and ju-jitsu, where you can spar with others, are also great. I am thankful that growing up, I had an interest in karate. This later branched into my adult life, where I encountered moments where self-defence was necessary and criminals could be detained until police showed up.

The legendary boxer Mike Tyson was one of the best of his time when he was champion. Growing up was a different story. He got bullied as a child and was even locked in the boot of a car. In a podcast of his, Mike mentioned how he regrets not being able to beat up the person who did that to him. If you have encountered violence in the past or been a victim of violence, be strong enough to forgive yourself for feeling little in that past scenario. Don't seek revenge. Know that it has shaped you into who you are today and who you are becoming. The rest of us can only imagine growing up and experiencing unpleasant moments of violence or physical abuse. It is definitely a big deal. However, believe you can change moving forward.

An excellent example is Oprah Winfrey, who was sexually abused as a teenager and even raped. After becoming pregnant at age 14 and losing the baby, as it was premature, Oprah did not let her past define who she had to become or be someone subservient. Oprah is a very powerful force in the celebrity world and has used her show as a platform to encourage people to get through their struggles. Be an Iron Mike Tyson or a bad-ass Oprah!

No one deserves to suffer physical violence. Therefore, I conclude this segment with advice to take self-defence classes or punch a punchbag or a bag of rice, whatever it may be. Don't punch your friends or family for practice, please! Gain the confidence of being comfortable with being violent and aggressive in a *highly controlled manner.* Remember, this can be another level of awareness.

Concluding the Journey of Confidence

Imagine you are going to work every day or a gym class every day where you haven't quite got the energy you desire. The simple fix is to eat a bit of food before you go or find that extra time in preparing for the day. Mentally, these steps make you feel more in control of yourself. Physically, you are less stressed; therefore, your blood pressure is not going into overdrive, which can assist anyone with anxiety/depression.

This is a simple yet effective example, but I am sure there are other aspects you can relate to in your own lives or changes you would like to make. Do something new. It's as simple as that, and you will thank yourself. With all these techniques and simple changes, you will find that you feel different and want to do things differently on your own terms.

This all translates into confidence. You know where you are going, you know why you are doing things a certain way, and no one is going to bring you down because you are too focused on your own self. Confidence-building, my friends, starts with small changes.

Confidence is the truth we know about ourselves, which we share with the rest of the world when the time is right. The best part is, it's like a muscle, and it never stops getting stronger. Keep at it, and you will constantly be gaining new forms of confidence through life.

The older you get, the more you will know about certain limitations. You may not be able to run as fast as you used to when you were 20 years old or as strong as you were. However, if you are aware of this, it does not have to become something to fear or avoid. You can plan from now how you wish to be in twenty years. The healthy food choices and exercises you do will benefit you twenty years into the future.

You will only forget your confidence if you do not continue to reinvent yourself throughout life. Carry this confidence you have discovered within you forever and rebuild yourself whenever you feel it is time to do so. There are highs and lows in life we'll have to face as we grow older. But the five-step technique can always place us back on the path. The confidence of handling life is what will keep us all on the confident track.

We are now on the way to becoming the golden bullet!

CHAPTER 8

Relationships

Romantic Relationships

Romantic relationships are pivotal points in many people's lives that can make or break them if they are not careful. Losing yourself, which I pointed out at the beginning of this book, is highly noticeable in this chapter of our lives when we become romantically involved with another person and connect with the wrong match. As you read on, and you read the word *love*, it is not just about loving relationships; it applies in the dating phase too. The cliché of loving yourself is something I never used to understand when I heard it, but as years went by, I learnt what it actually meant.

There are many people I have come across for whom losing-yourself mentality has kicked in. It's all to do with the imagined perceptions of one another. If you give too much of yourself in the relationship early on, this can be too much from one side. If the other person is not in the same mentality as you are, that individual is not ready to emotionally open up.

My two friends, who we shall call Steve and Pat, were in a relationship. Both lost themselves over time, as Steve did not love himself enough to put any of his needs forward. Pat and Steve would constantly argue. Steve at the time was always doing things to please Pat. Pat would constantly criticise Steve and start an argument.

I watched this relationship evolve over time. Steve always used to complain to me and our group of friends about how he could not be bothered anymore with the relationship. Pat was emotionally available, and she demanded the same from Steve. From what I could see at the time, Steve was not emotionally available, as he was still finding out who he was at the time. The emotional demands Pat was placing upon Steve were too much.

I could tell Steve wanted out of the relationship. He could not understand why they were arguing so much. Pat was getting frustrated and wanted to confront all of the bottled-up feelings in their relationship. When you look at it from this perspective, it is clearly a matter of not understanding each other and not being in the same headspace. However, when inexperience is involved, things can get messy.

Steve ended up cheating on Pat, and he felt very guilty afterwards. This was his big lesson at the time—that he was not loving himself enough to create a boundary in a relationship that Pat was controlling. Pat was not loving herself enough and was attempting to exert control over the relationship. She was insecure that she would lose Steve if she didn't take control.

I have seen numerous relationships that have not worked out, and it always has to do with insecurity in the relationship. This is not a bad thing, as people are still finding themselves and who they are. A healthy relationship can uplift both people and help them work through those insecurities together. This is all about keeping from losing ourselves in the first place and maintaining the relationship dynamic by consistently working on yourself and encouraging your partner to do the same.

Having a bulletproof mindset of self-belief creates value you place on yourself so you feel confident and secure in your relationship with another. When strong feelings of love are present in a relationship, it is very easy to become sensitive to your partner, as you expect your partner to be with you. The key word in that last sentence everyone should take away is *expect*.

Expectations from your partner is something you want to avoid. Imaginary bullets of expectations will only lead to disappointment. More importantly, it will put you on edge to have this constant expectation from your partner.

The best gift given to me in the form of advice was to love people for who they are. That's what is required. It's acceptance. This way, even though you may have differences in interests or viewpoints, that doesn't mean you can't be in love with each other. If you are truly confident within yourself and place a high value on yourself, you can accept your partner's differences. You complement one another and keep the relationship dynamic. If you have similar interests, that's great! But you can also lose yourself in this respect when you are not growing as a person and expect the other person to be exactly like yourself.

To recap, there are two elements here. If you are fairly opposite in terms of interests, respect and love each other for who you are. Avoid the control element of attempting to change one another. If you are very similar to your partner, don't have the expectation that this will remain throughout your life together. Your partner may want to grow in another area, and you should respect that. For yourself, too—you may see a new area to grow in which was not present at the start of your relationship. The value you place on yourself is the key to remaining in your power and keeping that bulletproof mind. The mind in control keeps emotions in check.

The emotions that stir in you from being dissatisfied by your partner not meeting your expectation is what will ultimately create bullets you do not need. The anxiety or depression felt when you are not in your power can take over your relationship and put you on edge. Don't fall for what you want the other person to become. You must realise from the beginning who your partner actually is. It's easy to spot this but harder to accept the reality. This is where taking a step back is highly important for yourself, not just the relationship.

The best way to keep your bulletproof mind whilst being in a relationship is to let everything unfold naturally, without any force. When a flower is growing, you do not ask it to hurry up. It blossoms at its own pace, and when it does, the relationship between the flower and time results in a strong, beautiful flower that unravels all of its petals at the right time. Flowers are part of nature, and nature is perfect. Relationships are part of nature. Don't let an imaginary bullet destroy your flower. The flower symbolises your relationship.

Dating

To briefly touch on this topic: the same method applies. Build yourself up before attempting to connect with another. There may have been times where you were emotionally available to connect with another and that person was not on the same page as you. You may be ready to settle into a relationship whilst the other person is not. I have been on both sides of the coin. I wasn't ready to settle down with a girl and she was; I was too focussed on my career. Another time, I was ready and the other person was not.

Ultimately, this causes chaos between you two, because you are not on the same page. The last thing you need is to hurt each other or have relationship anxiety. It's about recognising it before it happens. Therefore, I encourage taking time to get to know someone and that person's intentions if you are looking to eventually settle down.

Does your potential partner seem to be putting in as much effort as you? Is it too one-sided from you or one-sided from them? In observing the actions of the other person, you'll be able to see if it feels right or not. The real test of self-love comes when you are ready to walk away from a relationship you don't feel is right when in the dating stage. Or are you going to stick around to see if it will change? Before you attempt to get out into the dating world for something serious, have a look at the chapters about self-love.

If you are both looking for casual fun, then set that tone from the beginning. This way, no deep feelings are involved. If you have ever been disappointed in the dating world, where you thought it was all smooth and good between you two only to discover it's not what you really wanted, the worst thing you can do is attempt to fix the other person or the relationship.

The stepping-back element is highly important so you don't become entangled in the other person's bullshit. You are not a therapist or a parent figure. Bite your bullet and move on.

Being too nice in the dating world can sometimes come across as needy. Neediness doesn't project love. This is not to be confused with being mean in order to protect yourself. What this means is being *real*.

You are not being nice to impress the other person; you are being nice in the form of kindness and respect. No one needs to become a doormat in the dating stages in order to gain approval. True self-love will always be about being truthful with who you are as a person and making your truth clear.

If you are busy when you are not seeing your partner, genuinely *be* busy and have your time filled with developing yourself or activities you enjoy. Hold the space for the dating/relationship part, and you'll enjoy the other person's company even more. You'll in turn have a better time too. This is true self-love in the dating world and the relationship stages too. The rest of the time, hold a space for yourself. Being nice can come across as fake. The light teasing of each other is what'll create the excitement and suspense that adds to the attraction.

If you can cast your mind back to when you clicked with someone else, you'll find there was an element of banter. This banter lets you both have that enjoyment factor. It's because you are not worried about what the other person thinks of you, and you are both being in the moment. This is the difference that needs to be recognised about being nice in a fake way and being yourself in an engaging way.

The old saying of "be yourself" in the dating world means letting the other person discover elements about you and vice versa. You don't need to blurt out your qualities and what you are about unless it comes up in conversation. It is not an interview.

This will benefit you both and let things unfold naturally, and you'll avoid being taken advantage of. Equally, you'll respect the other person enough to not take advantage. True self-love is about treating the other person with respect; the value you place on yourself, you place on others too.

Whatever it is you want, you must know yourself through self-love. Self-love will help you recognise what you want from others, as you know what you want from yourself. The self-awareness will enable you to realise who you are as a person and what type of personality and energy you would like to associate yourself with and potentially connect with on a deeper level.

Relationship with Yourself

I have led with romantic relationships as a means of opening your eyes to how important and wonderful a relationship with another can be, with this closeness in dating or feelings of love for one another as the relationship develops. This is a real measure of how accepting we are of ourselves and how much we want to give ourselves to another person, not through fear but through feeling secure and allowing this to flourish.

You'll find as your relationship with yourself improves that you may not want to seek answers externally from others to gain validation. You'll start enjoying the small details in life and automatically want to expand your social network. Within that, you'll start recognising who is right for you too.

What we are going to delve into next is the relationship with yourself and how this affects your perception of the world around you. Simply looking at ourselves will establish how healthy and connected we can be with those around us, whether family members, work colleagues, friends, or anyone else we consider having a relationship with. Strangers are part of the mix as well. That short interaction you have with someone on the bus, maybe when giving up your seat to someone less able to stand, is a form of relationship. When you are confident in your own power, you are able to treat any other member of society the way you treat yourself.

Have you looked at yourself in the mirror up close and asked, "How are you?" If you do this and say it out loud to yourself in the mirror, you may be surprised by the reaction and feeling you get. You will feel like you are connecting with yourself. Asking yourself if you are OK is stronger than another person asking you. You are making time for your own well-being.

Are you putting others before yourself? Is that really healthy for you and the other person? There are many people who are very giving, and this is the quality of an angel. However, if you do this for too long, the angel wings will tire out and won't be as effective as they can be in looking after others. If you are not nurturing your relationship with yourself, how are you going to give your best to the people around you?

For those in a field of work where physical, manual work is required, if you are not looking after your physical well-being outside of work, what will happen to you if you injure yourself? You will become of no use. A lot of workers who are currently in their fifties and sixties have experienced discomfort in their body, as information about preventative measures for looking after muscles and joints was not always as highly available as it is today. The gym and fitness culture that millennials and Generation Z have grown up with has educated us on how we can keep health and fitness at the forefront of our lives. Some from the baby boomer generation have had to undergo knee surgery from years of heavy lifting, and physiotherapy for shoulder injuries from being at a desk for too long typing.

For those who value themselves in this type of scenario, the courage to speak up to your boss and say you're not feeling 100 per cent is important, as you are putting yourself first. You are not being a hero by hiding a pain. At the end of the day, your workplace will appreciate you, depending on what type of boss you have. But everyone is replaceable. Therefore, by realising your high value, you can prevent yourself from being treated any less.

Thankfully, most workplaces today are very supportive in terms of employee well-being. This is great progress within society as a whole when these factors are taken into consideration. Physical and mental health awareness has been highlighted a lot, and ways to cope with or prevent injury and mental stresses are available. The assistance may be available, but when employees are feeling really down in life, how many are reaching out for these services? This poses another question of how much self-care a person is willing to take on.

Many scenarios affect our adult life. Adults who were abandoned as children feel a void in their lives and can subconsciously feel they are not enough. There have been examples of this, particular with upbringings that have made them resilient in life and high achievers to prove to themselves that they are good enough. The deeper work ahead lies in how they feel away from their achieving side.

In situations of adults who were bullied as children, their self-worth can be low, as they may feel they were also not good enough. There was one high achiever I came in contact with who made his life a success materially and in his career. However, the deeper work still needed to be cleared, as it was affecting this particular individual in terms of the bullying he had been through. At the age of 32, although he appeared successful, he was not able to accept what took place in his childhood years. The memory still reduced him to tears.

Another scenario is when individuals have had their trust broken by a friend, romantic partner, business partner, etc. People are quick to place the blame on themselves first.

What has all this got to do with self-love? Everything. As I have learnt, when you love yourself, you keep yourself from becoming entangled in such situations in the future. More importantly, the self-love discovery enables you to put demons to rest from your past. The confidence steps have opened the door for you, and this should motivate you to take action in your life. The self-love element will further reenforce how you want to enjoy the rest of life.

What appears on the outside or on social media is not generally the real state of an individual. Take the example of Hollywood actor Robin Williams, who appeared really happy in public and would uplift others all of the time with his jokes. No one would have ever suspected someone as happy, famous, and wealthy as Robin Williams would even have thoughts of suicide.

Gary Speed, the footballer who committed suicide in 2011, was at the time the Wales National Coach. Wales was ranked 117 in the FIFA rankings. In December 2011, FIFA gave Wales an award for Best Movers of the Year, being ranked 45th. Speed was obviously doing well with his managerial career for Wales. He had it all in terms of material wealth. He had a wife and two children. What he did not make peace with in his mind ultimately took his life.

The night before he took his own life, no one who was with him could tell anything was different or unusual with him. He watched a football match and enjoyed the rest of his night. The following morning, his wife found he had hung himself. Suspicions of his time as a teenager at a football club were a possibility, where there was a coach who sexually abused boys over the course of many years. Could this have been lurking in his mind? It certainly could have made an impact if it did. Speed never said anything about his teenage years and if he had been abused or not. Whatever made him want to take his own life, one thing is for sure: he was being too critical of himself.

The point of the examples above is that different factors can affect your mental state the older you get. It's about regaining your love for yourself and remembering that the actions of others by no means define you. Whether you have been dumped in a relationship, bullied, insulted by someone, or feel you failed at something, you can learn to love yourself and use this as fuel to move forward. You have one life. Are you going to let the actions of other people control it? Hell no!

It's time to take action. The action step below will get your mind expanding on how much you can really appreciate yourselves in a genuine, authentic way. You are asking yourself for all the answers and no one else.

Action Step: Self-Love

1. Make a list of what you love about yourself. The following are examples to get your mind going. You may want to use them. However, you may have loads more qualities.

    - I am a kind person.
    - I am good at learning new things.
    - I am a really creative person.
    - I am fun to be around.
    - I am a great parent.
    - I am a great role model.
    - I am good at drawing/painting.

2. Go over your list. For each point you have made, ask yourself, *Why is this?* Write your answer underneath the question. I have done for "I am a kind person":

> "I am a kind person"
> *Why is this?*
> Because I offer to assist people who are in need.
> *Why is this?*
> Because I look to uplift other people.
> *Why is this?*
> Because I have strength in myself, and if I see someone who is feeling low, I know I can uplift them.
> *Why is this?*
> I have the strength through having a strong mind and believing I am invincible.
> *Why is this?*
> Because I am resilient from a young age.
> *Why is this?*
> Because I was exposed from a young age to strong characters such as Superman.
> *Why is this?*
> Because Superman is strong and invincible, I was able to see this in myself.

This is actually a real example I have applied to myself. I do consider myself a kind person. I delved into this deeper with the question of *Why is this?* It brought up very interesting answers.

Type or write whatever comes to your mind straight away. You'll be surprised by the answers you come up with. Avoid placing comparisons to other people within your answers; have the focus fully on you and what you have done to possess this quality or how you encountered or developed this quality. If there was someone who have inspired you, then by all means, give that person thanks in your answer. Gratitude is a great frequency to tune in to that'll make you feel balanced and appreciative.

The next step is to ask *What now?* By asking this question, you are making a decision about what you want to do with this quality you have identified. Remember, it's all about action. The following continues my example:

> *What now?*
> I recognise I am a kind person because I am strong. I am proud of this and, when appropriate, I will share this quality to uplift others.

Once you have found the answer, ask yourself how you can use this quality about you to love yourself. This is key here, as you are discovering the reasons why you love yourself. In turn, it'll show you how valuable you are and what you have to offer. Always keep it positive, and only talk about yourself in a positive manner.

> *How can I use this quality to love myself?*
> I can use this quality of kindness to be kind to myself first in order to nourish my strength and remind myself I possess such a quality.

Go deeper into the question of the action step of how it will be done. This is the commitment.

> *How will I do this?*
> I will do this by making time for my goals and hobbies. This is important to me, as I want to achieve in my life and not let a year pass where I feel I could have done more. I will relax daily before the next working day. I will also be kind to my body with what I am eating and make a conscious decision of what foods I eat that are beneficial to my health.

The next question is the affect this will have on you and those around you.

> *What will happen when I do this?*
> By doing this, I will remain unaffected by the opinion of others, and this will be my truth. My truth is my freedom. Having freedom around others is the ultimate superpower, as I am able to accept everything as it is without having to change myself.

By taking the above action to answer this question, you encourage yourself to find solutions to how the quality you started off with can connect with everything and the impact it will have, not only on those around you but on yourself. This is all about you finding why and how you are a great, lovable person.

Repeat this process for each quality you have listed about yourself. Answer all of them and see how amazing you feel by the end of it. Do one per day if you want to spread it out a bit, or do them all in one go. This is a positive emotional journey and will require thought and energy—in a good way, of course. When you stick at it and truly believe everything you are writing about yourself, you'll feel the affect rejuvenate you and give you newfound energy. It's better to let it happen naturally than attempt to force the answers.

More importantly, believe it. Keep encouraging yourself daily. In order to get the results we want, we must be consistent at it and check in with ourselves daily. The feeling of progress that we make with our goals and then fall off track for a week can turn into two weeks, then a month. This is what causes the cycle of feeling down in the dumps. We will feel like we have failed, all because we let the time escape us and did not continue with something we had started.

Buy a diary and write in it daily if you feel that will assist you in staying on track. Review what you love about yourself daily, and write in your diary how you applied this in a situation throughout the day. You are the best person to motivate yourself. You are the best cheerleader for yourself.

Conclusion

The topic of relationships with others can be a whole book in itself. The main aim here is that we come first and are the most important relationship to have with ourselves. Discovering that you can love yourself will make you a lovable person, as you will feel different when you are interacting with others.

As a reminder, being too nice in pleasing others is something we want to avoid. We want to be nice out of respect and acknowledge the values of the other person regardless of what type of relationship it may be—friends, family, romantic partners, etc. Knowing you are a diamond has power in itself, and your interactions with others will be of higher value, in a non-arrogant way that conveys through your body language and your sincerity that you are fun to be around.

Remember one thing: a glimpse of a diamond is enough to spark curiosity in the mind of others. Reveal your personality traits over the course of time as opposed to advertising who you are on a billboard to say, "Look at me." Be cool, calm, collected, and in control of yourself through the qualities you have discovered about yourself that make you a loveable person. And as a final reminder to truly make this life-changing, be consistent with sticking to your daily work of recognising your loveable qualities through journaling or a diary entry every day. Watch how the confidence and love shine through in all your interactions.

When you are confident and loving to yourself, the authenticity shines through when you interact with others. Putting on a front or trying to change yourself to match another person happens where self-love is absent. You are also the prize.

CHAPTER 9

Your Relationship with Time

Looking after yourself first is not a selfish trait. It is the value you have of yourself. A selfish, negative attitude would be a win-lose situation, where you put yourself first in order to receive the best whilst the other person receives less than you. This can be seen in something as simple as sharing an evenly cut bar of chocolate. If you wanted to take more than the other person in a manner of greed so you have more, this is not valuing yourself but devaluing yourself, as you are making the other person lose out.

There are many scenarios you have possibly been in where you have found yourself witnessing selfish behaviour by an individual, or you could be one of these people yourself. Valuing yourself is the starting point and further strengthens the bulletproof mind.

You may find that the more confident you become, the more people will demand your time. Call it what you want—whether it's people being attracted to your light, aura, or positive energy—there is something about your self-confidence that shows the value you place on yourself. When something or someone is of high value, it attracts a lot of attention.

This is not hippie-type, metaphysical nonsense talk. This is real; we see it all the time. Why are certain people able to naturally get on with those they meet? It is not by mere chance that they are able to connect with individuals by just being a likeable person. The mind you create of high value for yourself shapes your character and thus gives you a boost of energy within yourself so that you are able to converse with anyone you come into contact with.

This spark of positive energy within you can be felt by those around you. If you are feeling down and out, the people around you will notice your demeanour and how you are behaving. That slow, stalling feeling of heaviness inside will have that effect on those around you, and they are less likely to want to be around you.

This can sound like a harsh reality or an empowering reality. The empowering reality is that you are able to shape your mindset of destroying imaginary bullets you are creating within your head without questioning whether people are judging you or not. A lot of people do not realise how much you can actually achieve within a limited amount of time.

I have had those days where I am sitting at home, and I wake up late and watch TV. Then, as the time is passing from the clock on the wall, I am looking on TV listings to see what to watch next. On top of that, I had time fillers in between commercials where I would be looking at my social media or replying to WhatsApp messages to keep up to date with what is going on. There is no time for myself in these moments. It is an illusion that I am free with my time on my day off. In reality, it was a prison created for myself at the time. I was constantly keeping my mind stimulated for the sake of filling time.

When I have my plans set out of what I want to achieve, I am able to accomplish multiple tasks. It is really enjoyable and satisfying. The feeling you get when accomplishing your checklist is empowering. This is where the bulletproof mind comes into play, where you are not distracted and don't allow habit to take over your actions for the day. Habit can be destructive; you can be trapped in a zone of drifting through each day without progressing in any aspect.

The Value of Time

How you value time is how you value yourself. My friend mentioned earlier, called Steve, had changed his life around for the better when he began his growth-mindset journey. Steve and I attended meditation/growth-mindset classes. I remember one day in particular where Steve was at a crossroads with his life. He had to confront the feelings of resentment he had towards his father, who left home when Steve was a child.

The session that day lasted two hours. It was a special session where the head of the whole organisation, who is an energy practitioner, came down and hosted. He encouraged Steve to confront pent-up feelings, and Steve's conflict with his father was revealed. Something had to be done to bridge the gap between them.

That evening, after the meditation session, Steve went to see his father, who lived fifteen miles away. In the time he was with his father, they reconnected in an attempt to bridge the distance between them. After that, Steve also went to see his girlfriend. On his way back, he spoke to me on the phone, informing me about the events that took place. This all happened over a six-hour time period, from 6 p.m. to midnight. What he accomplished within those six hours was a massive confirmation for me that so much meaningful achievement could bedone.

Steve turned up on his dad's doorstep out of the blue and cried in his dad's arms, stating that he wanted to become close to his father. Prior to this, two years had gone by when he did not speak to his father much. In that time with his father, he cleared his own baggage and confronted feelings he'd hidden at the back of his mind and heart for so long.

After that, he saw his girlfriend. He wanted to spend quality time with her, and he did. He then had the time from his positive evening to speak to me on the phone and review what had happened. I was very happy to inform Steve that in six hours, he had accomplished a lot. This was not only a victory for that day; this was a long-lasting victory. And it all came from Steve's action of getting off his ass and attending a meditation session that evening.

Originally, Steve was not going to attend. He was feeling that his energy had been scattered throughout the previous two weeks. He was questioning his own growth mindset and why he was doing everything. This is something a lot of you may be doing at present in terms of what do you want to do or who you are as a person. There is more to you than you realise.

Steve is a perfect example of how to bite a bullet you've created, which in his case was procrastination. He confronted that within those six hours and changed his life forever. The value Steve placed in those six hours was the value he had in his actions. Had he not valued himself at that moment when he was sitting at home before meditation, he might have simply carried on watching TV and sat there till midnight. Instead, he took action steps forward to fight the procrastination. He went against it to create the reality of meaningful relationships that he longed for. Those six hours Steve experienced that night are something I will never forget. I often think about that night to remind myself how valuable time is when we value what we all truly deserve—the best.

In our meditation group, we share important moments on a WhatsApp group as a reminder and review of how we felt. With Steve's permission, I will share with you what he wrote on our group that evening:

> Wow … today was absolutely amazing … I can't even explain how I feel and how today has helped me address possibly the biggest issue in my life!
>
> So I went to go and see my dad straight after meditation as I felt in my soul to do and speak with him and express to him how I feel.… I called him and went to meet him, upon seeing him, I hugged him and just starting crying and felt so much love, joy and release that I be there with him in that moment. (He was obviously confused and shocked.) I told him that I love him and I expressed that I wanted us to have a proper relationship and move forward! … I also saw my grandparents who I hadn't seen in years which was an added bonus which also helped let go of some stuff I was holding onto. I know now that I have to maintain this relationship and nurture it also if I want to continue in my path.… I can honestly say I feel soooo light and full of love in this moment.… I want to thank you all soooo

much for such an amazing experience and meditation! Honestly a life changing 2 hours!

Steve put three red hearts at the end of his message.

How much value do you place on yourself now that you can appreciate the moments of time in the day to accomplish what you want to do with your growth mindset?

Action Step: Working with Time

It is easy to accomplish your goals when you have the following framework:

1. Brainstorm what you would like to achieve.
2. Select the goals you would like to accomplish within the next six months.
3. Break down the weekly routine required to complete these goals from Monday to Sunday.
4. Within those days, set yourself the time you are going to tackle a task.

The below table is an example of a person who wants to attend gym four times a week, eat more fruit and veg, increase water intake, practice drawing, meditate daily, spend time with family, watch TV less, and have eight hours sleep daily. This is simply an idea of how a person is able to set out the week whilst working a nine-to-six job Monday through Friday.

Sticking to the set times places accountability upon yourself that you are going to stick to your schedule. This is a personal schedule, and it is also possible to set a schedule for your working week too, to incorporate work tasks you have to achieve, and spreading it out over the working week as opposed to completing as much as you can in one day.

Time	Monday	Tuesday	Wednesday	Thursday	Friday	Saturday	Sunday
6-7	Shower/eat	Shower/eat	Shower/eat	Shower/eat	Shower/eat	Sleep	Sleep
7-8	Meditate 30 mins	Meditate 30 mins	Meditate 30 mins	Meditate 30 mins	Meditate 30 mins	Sleep	Sleep
8-9	Work travel	Work travel	Work travel	Work travel	Work travel	Shower/eat	sleep
9-10	Check work emails 20 mins	Check work emails 20 mins	Check work emails 20 mins	Check work emails 20 mins	Check work emails 20 mins	Meditate 30 mins	Shower/eat
10-11	Eat fruit/veg	Eat fruit/veg	Eat fruit/veg	Eat fruit/veg	Eat fruit/veg	Gym	Meditate 30 mins
11-12						Eat fruit/veg	Iron clothes for week
12-13	Eat fruit/veg	Eat fruit/veg	Eat fruit/veg	Eat fruit/veg	Eat fruit/veg	Wash car	Eat fruit/veg
13-14	Drink water	Drink water	Drink water	Drink water	Drink water	Shopping	Practice drawing
14-15	Drink water	Drink water	Drink water	Drink water	Drink water	Shopping	Family time
15-16	Eat fruit/veg	Eat fruit/veg	Eat fruit/veg	Eat fruit/veg	Eat fruit/veg	Family time	Family time
16-17	Drink water	Drink water	Drink water	Drink water	Drink water	Football on TV	Family time
17-18	Travel home 18:00	Travel home 18:00	Travel home 18:00	Travel home 18:00	Travel home 18:00	Football on TV	Family time
18-19	Reach home 18:30; catch up with family	Reach home 18:30; catch up with family	Reach home 18:30; catch up with family	Reach home 18:30; catch up with family	Reach home 18:30; catch up with family	Practice drawing	Family time
19-20	Gym	Gym	Practice drawing	Gym	Family time		Family time
20-21	Catch up with family	Catch up with family	Catch up with family	Catch up with family	Meet friends	Date night	Plan the next week
21-22	Reading 30 mins	Reading 30 mins	Reading 30 mins	Reading 30 mins	Meet friends	Date night	Sleep 22:30
22-23	Sleep 22:30	Sleep 22:30	Sleep 22:30	Sleep 22:30	Meet friends	Date night	Sleep
23-24	Sleep	Sleep	Sleep	Sleep	Sleep	Sleep	Sleep

The above timetable is simple, but it can keep a person on track. The bulletproof mind will not be shaken by breaking away from a personal schedule that has been created. If there are social occasions to attend, these can also be placed into the working week for an individual to work around. This way, your mind is structured for what you want to achieve.

Again, this is a simple tool to use and may not be for everyone. Some people are not ready to structure themselves and like to live life without plans. However, if you are serious about your goals, you are going to take steps to manage yourself. The above table sets out times to drink water on the hour and what time to attend gym. You do not need someone else to manage your life for you and set you your own life goal plans. Bite the bullet you have created of *not enough time*. This is creating your time. You can go into as much detail as you may wish and break down the timings by every half hour or every fifteen minutes if you must.

If you have children, this is the perfect tool to manage yourself and all your kids' activities, from after-school clubs to doctor visits. Manage yourself, and you will master time.

Your mind will adapt to this way of thinking to be as productive as you can be. You will be building blocks of encouragement for yourself as you feel a sense of accomplishment by doing this. All that we ever look for in life is a template to follow. Without a template, we are chasing our thoughts and second-guessing what we should do next. This is where you must bite your bullet and take action.

Tried and Tested

The above table is something I had to innovate for myself when I had a team of nine members of management underneath me. I had been part of a large management team myself when I was a department manager, and the way the general manager and his two deputies used to run the team was very competitive. You had to fight for your time or end up working ten- or twelve-hour days. This was not good for mental and physical health or for team building. It was a very old-school way of working together: work yourself flat until you have achieved what you have to do.

I used to make the same sort of table as above for activities that needed to be completed during the week. Instead of having just my name there, I would have all of my management team's names on the left-hand side. If there were one-to-one meetings they had to conduct with their own teams within their department, I would be sure to organise our week ahead by stating what date and time we would allow each manager to complete that task without overlapping another manager's time. This proved successful in giving managers work-life balance; keeping them from overworking themselves; and assisting with their development by allowing them to learn how to plan.

I was able to adapt any extra work thrown down from the head office into my framework for the week. Coming back to the phrase, "Manage yourself and you will master time," you could also say, "Manage yourself and you can manage others." If you cannot manage yourself, you will not be able to manage or lead the members of your team.

This can apply to your family too. If you have kids, you have to manage your own time as well as theirs. It is a tough job being a parent. Especially in the modern age we live in, there are many pressures on parents. Using this simple planning tool of managing yourself and your kids will definitely lift a weight off your shoulders and allow you to feel confident and in control of yourself. It allows you to confront all of what you have to face every week, and you will be able to tackle each situation head on.

Conclusion

In concluding this chapter on relationships, I want to make you aware that the relationships you have with yourself, partners, friends, colleagues and anyone else you are communicating with all boil down to your relationship with time. Your time will be high-quality if you value your own self and your own sense of time.

To highlight again, work on your relationship with yourself before anything else and realise you have so much value in who you are that the time you give to others is precious and valuable. By managing your time, you are managing your precious energy. The people you choose to spend time with will be worthy of who you are as a person.

CHAPTER 10

Energy Management

You are aware of the value you have and how you can grow through managing yourself. It is now time to become aware of how you manage your energy and focus to remain in a high constant state—and equally, when you need to relax and decompress.

How many times have you been in situations where you are drained by another person speaking negatively or complaining about circumstances that are out of your control? For example, people may complain about what they have heard about another person. Gossiping about a person is judging the other person against one's own set of values. This is why you should surround yourself with people with your same growth mindset.

If you have your plan set out for you, like in the table about managing your time from the previous chapter, this should assist you in managing your energy, as you are constantly evolving into a developing being. Energy management has a heavy amount to do with how much time you spend with quality people and what you expose your mind to. When I say *quality people*, I mean people who assist you in expanding your mind and are open-minded too. This does not mean you stay away and hide from people who are not goal-oriented. This is far from the point. The point is that how much time you allocate to people should be taken into consideration.

There are people I knew in college whose only interest was smoking cigarettes, eating chocolate, and talking negatively about other successful students who were "geeks." The energy I felt at the time was one of waste. I was all about succeeding, and the wasted energy I felt at that time made me want to stay away from that group. I knew this on an innate level, but I wasn't as aware as I am today of how to act on that feeling. There were days I would come home and feel I had wasted the day being around those people for two hours.

Contrast that to friends I had who were achieving their gym goals. This made me feel part of something bigger than myself, as I was growing into something new—not just in a physical sense with working out but that whole energy shift was appealing. You simply know this on an innate level.

See how you feel in certain situations. Your body will not lie to you. You may get this feeling in your gut that something is wrong, or you will feel heavy and lethargic around someone who seems to be surrounded by a lot of negative drama. You will only feel this when you yourself are living your true path.

The bulletproof mind is aware of who is attempting to slow it down and who is assisting it on a win-win level. If you win, the other person should win too. There is no win-lose scenario. If you are being pushed in the gym by friends to lift weights, then you will encourage them to win with their gym goal as well. For those of you who have been in this position, you will know that psychological edge you feel when you both are achieving together and bouncing off each other's energy.

Another scenario can be studying for an exam, where you avoid studying through procrastination. This brings your energy level down. If your friend is wanting to avoid studying and watch social media or go out clubbing instead, and brings you to that level, you have to be strong enough to know your value and expend your energy in the correct places. If you don't want to study, that is your decision, but ultimately how you pump your own energy up is down to you, and the bulletproof mind finds this possible to achieve. Even more fulfilling is the reward of prioritising what is important, such as studying, and then going clubbing!

Procrastination was highlighted towards the beginning of this book, and it is one of the regrets that will be felt in old age by a large amount of the global population. You know when you are procrastinating because you force yourself to do something easy—watching TV, replying on social media, scrolling through social media, or calling friends when you didn't need to call them.

This doesn't just apply to studying. There have been occasions we can all relate to in life where we were invited out somewhere when really, we wanted to get important jobs completed at home or run errands. At times, we can avoid our responsibilities when a friend invites us out somewhere.

Another scenario can be when your job is looking to enrol you in more courses at your workplace. There is no right or wrong rule that you have to keep progressing in your workplace. If you want to be the best version of yourself, though, it is always a good feeling to continue growing in your role, which will assist you in your everyday life.

One friend I have who we'll name Amber put off enrolling in a course at her workplace for one year. She would complain now and again that she was finding things too easy at work. The opportunity to grow was something she never delved into. Yet she kept stating that she wanted to enrol in this course. When I'd had enough of Amber talking the talk without walking the walk, I had to offer her my thoughts on how she was hindering her growth by overthinking.

This energy management of mine was for myself too. If Amber did not like what I said, that was her problem. I value myself enough not to let my energy become flat as people consistently speak about how they are not doing something. As Amber is my friend, I was able to say to her directly what she needed to hear. Thankfully, Amber enrolled in the course the next day. She had been putting it off for over a year. This is a great example of how not letting anyone around you affect your energy and instead shifting the energy to a positive vibe can inspire another to achieve a goal to grow as a person.

Listen to your body and be confident enough to know who you are getting involved with, whether it be a romantic relationship or a friendship. As I have stated earlier, the value you discover within yourself is the value you place on the relationships around you. This in turn enables you to form meaningful relationships where another person cannot disrespect you to the point where you lose yourself, as mentioned so far throughout this book.

Be the value you see when you look in the mirror. If you are feeling low in value, you have to change that immediately by looking yourself in the eye and realising your true potential.

Action Step: Eye Gaze Exercise

Go to the mirror and get up close—I mean *really* up close. Look yourself in the eye and observe how you feel. You will be surprised at how elated and calm you will feel at the same time. There is only room for love when you look at your eyes up close. This is something I discovered over fifteen years ago.

There is one incident that happened where I advised someone about this technique. This person I knew was upset about a situation and began to cry whilst driving. All of a sudden, the mirror on the sun visor of the car was down, and this individual looked into it. Immediately, the crying stopped. Seeing yourself cry in the mirror reminds you that crying is unnecessary. It made this person stop and feel embarrassed about feeling so low.

There is nothing wrong with crying. It is a great release. However, when you get into that state, how long do you wish to remain like that?

My technique of looking in the mirror evolved. One day, I looked at my eyes in the mirror up close and just began to stare into all the intricate details of my eyeball—the colours around the perimeter of my eye, the different shapes seen around my pupil. I actually began to smile, too, as I became happy looking at my eye. It is amazing how you have the key to your own well-being. Instead of me saying *happiness*, I will say *mood*. Who knows if you will become happy looking deep into your eyes?

This is a valuable tip I share with you all. In staring at your own eyeball up close, you can regain your sense of power and self-belief, knowing you are trusting yourself when you do this. I am actually going to do this right now, after I have typed this sentence.

Positive Strength

What is positive strength? This is where you increase your positivity, which gives you an unlimited amount of energy and keeps you motivated to do anything. For those of you who have been down in your lives or even depressed, there is a feeling where you have no energy at all. You walk around and have this weight-like feeling in your stomach. You feel it in your eyes, where they are open but not present to your surroundings, and everything feels hazy.

This occurs, for example, when you lose someone close to you or feel disappointed by a situation you were not expecting to find yourself in. This is to highlight to you the contrast of how we can feel when we are down and a lack of energy we have in these moments. Now, on to the flipside, where we are full of energy and buzzing around everywhere. I appreciate that some people have not felt this before, which is why I wish for everyone to feel this way.

I have met people who have not experienced these moments of flow. They are missing the feeling that anything they do can only produce positive outcomes—also known as *flow state*. Through self-talk, speaking out aloud, or writing down affirmations of positive messages to yourself, you are literally creating energy inside of you. The feelings that are created inside you are optimism and decisiveness in meeting each moment of the day.

Action Step: Create Your Own Positive Energy

Write down on a piece of paper, "I am the best." Write it and believe it. These are moments where you are creating this energy. Other examples could be:

- I am full of life and love.
- I am the greatest powerful, positive energy in the universe.
- I bring joy to all around me.

- I can do anything.
- I am strong and powerful.

A good one I like saying daily is how I am going to make it a great day. "I am making it a great day," I say at the beginning of the day or if I am in the car driving. Setting the tone and correct intention for the day is important, as you are making the choice of how you want to live out the day. If you are down and out, and you have no intention for what you want to feel for the day, you will continue to repeat this on a daily basis.

Saying or writing down these positive thoughts creates this belief in yourself. And why not create this belief in yourself? Who is to say you are wrong for doing this? Who can tell you that you are not any of these aspects of life? Remember that no one is able to affect our bulletproof mind when we shape our thoughts and beliefs. That is the foundation to always remember: we are the one with the power for ourselves.

With affirmations and positive messages to yourself, you can feel anything you want to. Whatever you want to believe about yourself is up to you. Encourage yourself to take this action step and see how you feel after one sitting.

Remember from our earlier discussion about confidence-building that the small action steps we take create confidence and belief. This is a level-up where the energy inside will feel high. There is everything to gain by doing this, and all you need is a pen and paper and your own voice—which leads us on to the next phase of positive strength.

Action Step: Record Your Voice

Where you have your affirmations, say them to yourself. By this, I mean record yourself saying, "You are the best. You are the greatest."

Whatever it is you want to tell yourself, listen to yourself. Do you believe the words you are hearing? If not, record them again. How do you sound? Does your voice sound decisive or hesitant? This self-analysis will build your confidence levels and your energy levels. If you hear yourself sounding nervous or unsure, how does that make you feel? How you instantly feel is how others will feel in your presence. You cannot fake the power felt in your voice. It is something that will occur naturally the more you work on it, and your interactions with everyone will have a different vibe when you recognise this aspect of yourself.

We have all seen TV shows or a live speech where the speaker's words are so powerful that you feel them. Martin Luther King's speech was so decisive that people felt his words of power, which inspired belief in all. Do that for yourself. Inspire yourself and watch how you inspire those around you. Just from your belief in yourself, the words will carry power with them. Therefore, I encourage you to record your voice and speak to yourself for you to hear.

Take it up a level, if you must, and take a video of yourself. How are you holding and carrying yourself when you sit, walk, and stand? Place a camera on record and walk towards the camera. Is this how you walk? How are you feeling when you see yourself on video walking? Do you look like someone confident and approachable, or someone who doesn't feel comfortable approaching people or situations? Are you slouching when you walk? Is your posture reflecting the internal energy you are projecting? When you answer questions about yourself, it is highly important that you are brutally honest with what you see or hear.

How can we take power over our thoughts, ultimately preserving our energy and using it to progress? Analyse your thoughts. Are they thoughts that are wasting your energy? Thoughts like *Why am I not where I want to be?* or *I don't look good in this* or *I just want to go home* are there for a reason, but they are wasted thoughts equating to wasted energy.

If you have ever had that feeling where you cannot get to sleep and you are consistently thinking of moments that bother you, that is wasted energy. When you do eventually fall asleep, you wake up feeling tired, as you were running on adrenaline when you were kept awake. Write your thoughts down. Get them out of your head. Analyse them. Ask yourself why they have come up. It can be either a clearing thing to do or a chance to love the thought.

Study Yourself and You Will Know Yourself

Bite your bullet and do the above. If it is something you have never done before, it is time to start. You are self-reflecting and self-analysing even more, knowing more deeply who you are by the sounds and tones of your voice. The words you say and thoughts you think are a measure of your energy. Are you generally making positive statements throughout the day, or are you saying anything negative?

Scientists know more about space and planets than they know about the deep oceans on earth. Consider the earth and everything outside of you space. Go deeper into your own world so you know who and what you are. You will only discover the speeding golden bullet once you have found this energy along with extra confidence—positive strength.

Energy management is heavily around knowing who you are and what daily steps you take to create your new persona—not one that is faked but one that becomes you. I relate it to my own journey and that of others I know of who have changed their way of living through the personal growth journey they have undertaken. Then there are those I know who for twenty years have remained in the same mindset and procrastinated their lives away through living in their comfort zone. They behave at the age of 45 the same way they behaved at the age of 18 and then regret what they have become.

Energy management means utilising the fuel within to allow us to accomplish and attack each day on our own terms. Consistently taking this approach to living is something that motivates us, as we feel more in sync with life as opposed to merely existing. Physical fitness also assists in our energy levels, allowing the body to work in harmony with the mind.

This leads us on to the next chapter, as the way we motivate ourselves through energy management can be unlocked and inspired in another individual through leadership.

CHAPTER 11

Leading

The teachings from all previous chapters must be understood in order to grasp what is outlined ahead. A lot of inner work has been done leading up to this point. All the principles you apply to yourself can now work on a grand scale involving other members of your team or whatever group it is that you are leading or interacting with in your daily life.

Leading is important to a lot of people. But why is this the case? What is the reason you want to lead in something? Whether it be a task or an aspect of everyday life, what is your reason? For some people, leading can be a case of an ego trip. This kind of leading can be dangerous for all involved, as it does not benefit the majority. It can be a win-lose outcome, in which the leader in charge is the one feeling the best and happiest whilst others are not happy and look to the leader for a chance to feel valued. This is manipulation.

The theme of the previous chapters was preventing you from losing yourself. You can lose yourself by following another without having the feeling of growth involved. You may have been there yourself, where you are following orders but feel almost robotic and not present with what is going on around you. Engaged followers want to do their best for the leader by using their own brain to make decisions. Of course, the leader is there for guidance.

If you have ever placed yourself under the leadership of someone who demands blind following, you may begin to make mistakes. Blindly following a leader's orders is not enough, and it does not help the follower grow or feel empowered. This only occurs where the person has not been shown guidance correctly in the first place. Asking others to follow instructions to a tee will only make them robotic, and they will begin to make mistakes. With empowerment comes ownership. Ownership gives the individual freedom to take the reins, and this is where mistakes are minimised and a sense of purpose is felt.

Would you really want to lead a team of people who felt lost and undervalued because of you? I am sure the answer is no. Leaving a legacy with people you have led is something that happens naturally. It is not something you intend to do.

There is a moment I remember from my career where the head of HR held a meeting on people management. Her name was Lisa, and she was the head of HR for a very large company. She gave a talk regarding leading people and ways to handle different situations. There is one sentence Lisa wanted everyone to remember, and she would say it at the end of each of her sessions: "You may not remember everyone that you manage, but they will always remember you."

It is very powerful and true that the leader will always be remembered, whether the worker's experience is good or bad. It is evident that to be an effective leader, you must remain in your power and not lose yourself. A lost person leading will only confuse team members. Can a lost person lead a team? Sure, but the quality at which such a person leads could be detrimental to all.

Creating a team of leaders will enable them to lead you too. Yes, the leader can be led. If you believe the leader at the top never has problems to encounter, of course they do. We all do. In those times when a leader needs help from the team to deal with situations in their personal life, what happens? Whatever needs to get done will get done because of the leaders underneath. They in turn motivate the leader at the top, as they will be solution-focussed. This is the intention and energy set by you, the one who has done the inner work.

Setting an Intention

Biting our bullet creates the opportunities we seek to develop and progress through life. We are creating ourselves into leading ourselves.

Leading a team with an end common goal in mind is essential for creating a purpose for why everyone is working together. What intention do you want to set with your team? If you are a manager of a team, you are a leader. If you are a sports coach, you are a leader. If you have organised a social event with friends and family, you are a leader. If you are a parent, you are a leader. And I am sure there are numerous other examples of situations where a leader can be found and even created.

The formula for leading is very simple and includes the following:

- self-confidence and belief in the vision of the goal/target you want to achieve
- creating an environment of positive belief amongst the team (building belief in themselves)
- showing trust and value in each one of your team members
- recognising effort and input of individuals
- setting yourself and others up for success.

With this approach, what you will find is that the team is not following your commands. They are not robots. The team becomes inspired by wanting to have the best results.

A leader who communicates in a confident manner inspires the whole team. You cannot fake this confidence. If we have worked on all the clearing stages and built ourselves up with confidence from the previous chapters, our intention-setting with the team creates a standard that we set for ourselves and for those around us.

This can apply to many aspects of life. Leaders are found everywhere, and they may not realise it. Some people don't know they can be a leader until someone points it out to them. If you are a leader in a certain aspect of life, there will be a time when you have to be a follower. This does not mean that you are below in status. Far from it. Everyone has a time to lead. It depends on expertise in the chosen area.

For example, my mum can lead our family in baking a cake by directing people on ingredients to be purchased and what kind of methods are used to bake a cake. My mum may not realise this, but she can be a leader if she wants to be. Transferring these skills into other areas in life is possible.

Think about your own situation. Are you a worker in a company where you want to become promoted to a senior position? Have you ever thought about how you would lead a team and how the team members would respond to you? These are good questions to ask yourself before getting into that position, as it would mentally prepare you for what lies ahead. There may be imaginary bullets in your way, such as the following:

- How will the rest of the team respond to me when I was at their level and now I will be above them?
- What will happen to me if they don't listen to me?
- What if I fail?
- What if they hate me?

From my experience, you cannot please everyone when you are promoted. There will be colleagues who are genuinely happy for you and some who are not happy for you, for whatever reasons they may have.

However, referring back to what we've learned about confidence, this is what should keep you on track to be what you want to be regardless of other people. The opinions of others are none of our business. Our confidence within ourselves and the steps we have taken to confidence-build will deter any forces against us.

Once you radiate confidence and self-love as a leader, everyone around you in the team will be inspired, as you are leading and commanding from a place of authenticity. That authenticity is your true, confident self. It sounds very simple when reading back that last sentence, but that is how simple it will seem when you find yourself leading teams.

To mention once again my previous sentence of not being able to please everyone, that may be the case in the beginning. However, keeping team members in the loop on your journey and vision will help those people see you as an inspirational leader. This is achieved by not giving too much focus to the individuals who are showing you resistance. When you remain consistent with your vision of victory with your team, everyone who wants to believe in you will be inspired to do so. The resistant members will gradually come on board, or they will leave.

It is a win–win situation, as you will have the correct positive energies surrounding you. Any negative people on your team will fade away. The ones who are on your side should be encouraged and praised in private too. This will create the value. If you have any other negative thinkers in your group, the best way to deal with these people is the responding technique.

Reacting and Responding

For many years, I have observed leaders in all walks of life, including football coaches in teams I have played on, business owners, managers at different levels above me leading teams, and family members organising social events. There is one trait I have noticed that I have been able to craft into my own leadership—one that is very successful. I say this with confidence, as I have seen the difference in my leadership style. It has yielded great results.

Since going through my self-growth journey I have grown to learn this art of responding vs reacting. The reactive state is somewhat limited in terms of keeping team cohesion in place. Reactions have to do with acting on impulsive feelings and becoming offended by people challenging your authority.

Everyone has been there at some point in life, where another person has said something that has angered us in some way or made us feel an emotion that we did not want—sadness, rejection, disappointment, etc. What does this highlight about us that another person's words have so much power to make us feel a certain way? Why do you believe it to be true?

When I was first starting out leading teams, I was reactive. Any jab at my authority would make me want to show my might and not accept my authority being challenged. This I picked up off many old-school leaders I had worked under previously. Although it may have worked in my favour at the time, the outcome was not so pleasant in terms of how the environment felt after that. It was not productive in the long run for all involved. Again, thankfully, I was able to bridge the relationship with those involved. Getting into an argument with anyone by reacting to them only fans the flames and wastes energy. A more proactive approach taken thereafter was responding to situations.

I never knew anything about meditation. My perception of meditating was that it had to do with breathing, having eyes closed, and having no thoughts. There is an element of that. However, the truth of meditation is actually embracing our emotions and not by repressing them, but expressing emotions from a place of love as opposed to a place of anger. When we say *place of love*, it is far from being hippie-like with a flower in your hair. (Nothing against it if you want to do that.) *Place of love* literally means the inner work we have done on ourselves through *Bite Your Bullet* and living authentically.

When responding to other people's negative thinking, it is down to the leader to alter the energy by displaying an example of positive thinking. The self-confidence and belief we have in ourselves cannot be altered by another person's negative comments or thinking. This is not to be confused with being too stubborn with your team members and the points they make. You can use it to your advantage when a negative statement fuels you on to further cement the belief you have in your vision.

It is highly important to keep that belief atmosphere going within the team despite a small number of individuals being negative about what needs to be achieved. The example you are setting is one that becomes inspirational, as you are looking to achieve the big prize in your chosen field. Showing the team it is easy to achieve creates the belief. The hustle-and-bustle aspect of achievement is a myth that says you have to force the situation to achieve at the expense of yourself. When you truly show your team you enjoy what is being achieved, success becomes reachable.

An example of this that I have witnessed involves a resident of a nearby street. This individual had a situation where cars would drive on the grass verge, and it was ruining the grass, creating mud tracks which would spread everywhere. One solution this person came up with was placing a large rock in the way. This was not the best solution, as it would have caused damage to many cars if their car tyre had gone onto it—or worst yet, if it got caught under a car's bodywork, causing significant damage.

The local council was monitoring residents not looking after the grass verge by posting letters if the condition was not great. The next idea the resident came up with was placing a cone on the grass verge. The cone was small and not very noticeable. Again, there were incidents where the cone got caught under cars that were driving in, and it would get squashed.

After many months, the neighbour actually came up with a solution from a place of love. Whether it was intentional or not, it worked. The neighbour planted a small pine tree and flowers. These were positioned in the centre of the grass verge. The small arrangement captures the attention of pedestrians walking past to this day. I saw three children taking pictures with this flower arrangement when they stopped their cycling and sat next to the flowers to take pictures.

This place of love has kept cars from driving on the grass verge, as it is now viewed as more of a flower monument than a verge. A simple act of responding to the environment has yielded desired results. The grass verge is looked after without the need for cones or signs such as *Keep off the grass*. A sign like that is reactive. It challenges certain people to oppose cooperation and instead go against the sign to express their individuality.

Can you see in the example above the fluidity of the solution and the art of responding? The individual who made the flower arrangement did not need to fight tooth and nail with members of the public driving over the grass verge. Ultimately, individuals who find solutions like this remain in their power and do not lose it by reacting. They do this by creating a positive solution where, in this case, people are naturally led to respect the environment which was previously being damaged.

The same thing happens with our emotions. If there are situations you face with team members who are not behaving for the benefit of the team, coming from a place of authenticity is far more effective and nurturing than striking them down—within limits, of course. We are referring to situations that involve negative thinking, which could potentially bring down the whole team. Anything to do with illegal activities or rule-breaking of course must be responded to in the correct manner. That would not be tolerated within the team, and it is your job to set the boundaries.

However, you will find that when you are coming from a place of authenticity, team members are less likely to rule-break or go against the ethos of teamwork, as value within the team has been created. If team members respect you genuinely, as opposed to respecting you out of fear, they are more inclined to want to assist you in achieving the team goal. Create strong links and prevent weak links within your team.

An Example of Remaining in Your Power

Where you have a difficult team member who is challenging your authority or a difficult person to face in your everyday life, the best way to respond is to recognise that the other person is the one with an issue, not you. Where individuals project their negativity onto others, they are really talking to themselves. Do not fall into their power trap.

You must also remember that their reality is real to them. If they have a miserable outlook on life, address that from a place of authenticity. Remember the identifying, clearing, and confidence-building you have done with yourself; the same thing happens when you are leading a team member. Having a one-on-one conversation and displaying your authenticity is far more effective than attempting to argue your point of view.

An example I have encountered occurred when I went in to manage a team and was met with resistance from three members of the management team. The funny thing was, I came in super-positive and genuinely kind to everyone. The majority of the team was happy with me and on my side. The management team, however, was not happy with the positive outlook that was spreading through the store. Results began to improve, and areas of the store were becoming clean. Prior to my arrival, the store was ranked as one of the worst in the company, at 541/543, and the store had areas that were not clean.

A lot of the team members noticed the difference that was taking place and would inform me of how they felt proud that this was happening in their work environment. Yet one of the management-team members at the time wanted to argue with me. This individual's management colleague was nearby providing support. I was very surprised that the point of their argument was that I was using the internal radios a lot. I valued the radios for communication. But I knew there was more at play here, and it didn't have as much to do with the radios as the change in the store, which the management team was uncomfortable with.

There was a time when I might have engaged in a battle of words. But now, I listened to what was being said. I didn't react with anger but allowed the other person to speak. I purposely let that person finish speaking without interrupting. Finally, I asked what this person would like to change. There was no answer. I then asked if there was anything else. Again, there was no answer. The main goal had been to engage me in an argument. And I would not engage. I just reiterated that my intention in this store was to be positive with everyone and that we could be the best team.

After two weeks, those particular members of the management team resigned without any arguments having taken place between us or any dramatic episodes in the store. There were complaints about those particular members of management from the wider team, but thankfully for the whole team, the negative influences in the store had left. The atmosphere afterwards was very positive, and the team members who had worked there for a long time were finally happy with the atmosphere and direction of the store. New managers joined the store, and things flowed very well, for which I am grateful.

If I had argued back and reacted to those managers' words, I guarantee those negative thinkers would not have resigned, as my reaction would have fuelled their negative thinking. They would have enjoyed it. They would have stayed until they drove me out.

I know this to be true, as the leader who was there before me resigned after the same arguments and resistance. Unlike me, that leader reacted and left.

With a new management team in place and others getting promoted, the atmosphere in the store was the best. It rose to number 1 in South England and 4 in the whole of the UK, all through a positive atmosphere change. The power of responding works.

The point of the example above is that remaining in your power and authenticity allows you to act appropriately to the situation at hand. When you are authentic, there are no nerves inside you or any flustering moments. The worst thing you can think while travelling to work is *What is going to happen next?* or *I cannot be bothered to go into work today.*

All the negative feelings one may experience offer a chance to be corrected. It is a spinning imaginary bullet you do not need anymore. Discover a new power as you become a new version of yourself, leading others and leading yourself.

Action Step: Reevaluating Past Situations in Order to Grow

Remember that reactive situations are those where you have engaged in arguments or made decisions based on anger and frustration. It does not have to be in a work environment. It can be in any environment. Follow these steps to evaluate such situations:

1. List situations in your life where you have reacted in a negative way.
2. Once you have listed those situations, describe in more detail what happened.
3. What impact did each of these reactions have on you/and team? (if applicable)

4. What would you do in the same situation today?
5. What would the impact(s) be of the way you handle it today?

Responding to Everyday Life

Responding means accepting a situation has happened and moving forward whilst at the same time creating the solution with your response. How many times have you been in a situation where you have reacted with intense emotion, only for it to ruin and influence your whole day?

Let's take an imaginary example of you going out somewhere in the morning, only to have food spill on your top—say jam on toast. It could be a white shirt or a summer dress. Now you have a big jam stain. The reactive state of becoming angry at the situation or yourself has the potential to impact the rest of your day. You would drive around annoyed, tell people you know about how terrible your morning has been, etc. This spreads across to your whole day, and you end up blaming every negative thing that happened on this one incident.

How could you respond to this situation instead of react? Responding would involve accepting the fact that you have got this stain on your top. You would head back upstairs to change the top and carry on with your day. Sure, it might have been an item of clothing you purchased for a specific occasion, but the situation requires action so you can continue with your day ahead.

What you'll find is that after you have done the inner work from earlier chapters, you'll be more likely to respond. When people react, it's usually a projection of how they are feeling inside and taking it out on another person. Once all the clearing has been done, the responding comes naturally, as you are not led by emotion and are human enough to accept the present moment. Not being led by emotion does not mean becoming a robot with no feelings. It is appreciating life as the bigger picture. One small incident is not enough for you to feel overwhelmed.

There have been many situations like this with people I know, and myself in the past, where an incident impacts your morning and filters through the whole day. What we are doing when we react to situations that influence our whole day is create an excuse as to why we feel angry and frustrated. We use it as a justification to feel a certain way.

Instead, we are the ones who lose out, as our productivity in anything we have wanted to do diminishes. We end up telling people what happened. Do they care? Probably not. We are leaders of ourselves, and getting the sympathy vote from another person because we dropped jam on our shirt will only encourage that person to further fuel our frustration. This is how we create our reality. If you fuel another person with matters that are bringing you down, they will follow.

Instead, if you really want to mention it, talk about how you found a solution. Use it in your one-to-one session with your team as an example of remaining positive in all situations, for your own well-being and theirs also. If you need to vent in order to feel better, think of how the other person feels after you have vented. You may not realise it, but you do have an effect on other people as they absorb all of your troubles, which they were not ready for.

Venting to a trusted individual who is *ready* for a download of venting from you can work as long as you build yourself and the other person back up. Keep it positive always. I have watched very senior leaders visit their sub-leaders in different areas of the UK, and I have observed the difference a positive intention vs a defeated persona can have.

Leading by Positive Motivation vs Ruling by Fear

Whatever you do, don't rule by fear. Ruling this way highlights that you are in fear yourself. You are so insecure that you have to force decisions and manipulate another person's feeling. Deputies or general team members being manipulated by their leader is something I observe 85 per cent of the time. The distress in these individuals is very clear, but they do not see it themselves. They are bending backwards in order to impress their boss out of fear, not out of a positive end goal, too scared to make a mistake in fear of disappointing their boss.

Bosses who rule this way enjoy it, as they feel they have a lot of power. Sarcastic comments to constantly put others down is only a bullying attempt to make themselves feel further boosted. All of this I have witnessed first-hand as a visitor to many locations, observing how the leaders of the place conducted themselves with their team members.

The results of that environment spoke for themselves. The team did not care about the overall goal. Mistakes were hidden from the boss out of fear of a big episode taking place or a big drama. When you make another person feel on edge or fearful of making a mistake, that's mental harassment. Your team members lose respect for you, as they are so focussed on what can go wrong. You can bet they will feel like this in other areas of their lives if this is what is happening at work. Next time you see people in authority with their team, observe how the team members' body language and verbal communication is with their boss.

Leading with positivity has to be performed with the intention of feeling like a spark of energy anywhere you go. Walking amongst your team members and saying a simple hello will mean the world to them. Don't be one of those people who has to wait to be spoken to or feels that employees should come to you. You must take the first step by greeting them. This makes your team members feel highly valued. When you hold that respectful persona of invincibility with care, the rest of the world responds with admiration and just generally wants to be around you.

Confident leaders ensure that motivation is sparked in team members the moment they meet on that particular day. It should take no more than thirty seconds to get that drive and passion going. The team will begin to respect you and, in turn, will reciprocate that positive energy.

How do you show positive energy? The way you feel and walk should feel light—no dragging your heels around or looking down at the floor. Show your team the presence you possess by looking them in the eye, smiling if it comes naturally to you, fist-bumping each other, shaking hands, high-fiving, etc. All that makes a difference. If that is not in your personality, a simple two-minute conversation is all you need, and watch how productivity will increase from those individuals.

Situations of Responding

Responding means channelling your surroundings to create the environment you want. From all the examples above, it is clear that the channelling of situations can be used as a motivation to transfer it all into a positive. Whatever problem you may face as a leader, the answer is always in the situation.

Someone Being Difficult

Have a one-on-one meeting with difficult individuals and let them talk. It is very important to let them finish. Reiterate your positive goal and ask what support they would like from you. Let them come up with the answers. You may have to nudge them slightly into the clearing and rebuilding. If they are acting out of line with team members or even yourself, this is where the boundary-setting has to start. This can all be done in a calm manner, of course.

Not Achieving Targets

If your team is not making its targets, you can respond by brainstorming on paper how you can make it go right. The reactive state to this would be to get deflated about not meeting your goals. Your success will be exponential if you can respond instead. If you have not met targets or desired results, brainstorming and sharing your conclusions with your team will encourage their ways of thinking to become solution-oriented, as you are leading by example. They will most likely come up with a solution that will encourage you to act.

Reframing

Look at the way every situation can be reframed. This is true power and adapting to any situation that may present itself to you. Finding a positive in any negative situation allows you to always win and never fail. If you are generally a reactive person and feel this may not happen overnight, take these small steps of reframing situations as a tool to assist you in moulding yourself into a new powerful, controlled version of yourself.

We are fighting only with ourselves when we react. It's wasted energy if you are at war with yourself. When we respond, we find the solution, without the emotional reaction. The reframing tools below have to be done with a highly determined attitude. Attitude is the key here. Reeling off the words below is not enough. The feeling of determination and high belief in your own words spoken is what will guide you.

The following are examples of reframing:

- **Situation:** *Traffic on the road is making my journey home thirty minutes longer.*
  Reframe: *I'm safe and I have more time to myself. I'll call others to tell them I'll be late, enjoy the music, and de-stress instead of stressing at the situation.*

- **Situation:** *I didn't achieve my goal.*
  Reframe: *This is a perfect opportunity for me to get even better and research more how I will get there. I can evaluate how I was in the lead-up of missing my goal and make adjustments for next time.*

- **Situation:** *I didn't get the job I wanted.*
  Reframe: *A better opportunity is going to come.*

These are generic examples. How we create our fears is how we also create our faith—faith in ourselves, that is.

The mind wants to create the reality we believe. I cannot highlight enough that we make it happen. Remember that inner work clears out the baggage. The rebuilding is what gets opportunities knocking on our door, as we are interacting differently with the world and noticing good things in the world more than bad. It all makes a difference.

There is no such thing as rejection. If you have fully prepared for an opportunity and it does not happen, the worst thing you can do is beat yourself up over it. Remember to reframe it. When you know you have done all you can to prepare and you are feeling confident and at your best, and then you get a rejection, you are not the problem or issue, and you must believe that. The bulletproof mind does not get fazed by perceived setbacks. Instead of rejection, reframe it to redirection. You are being redirected to something even better.

Leading by example and implementing this does not have to be a big job. Get rid of the idea that it has to be a big deal or difficult. This is not the case. Believing this is easy to do is not unrealistic. The greatest thinkers in history came up with inventions when people thought they were crazy. Believe in yourself even when other people doubt you. Believe in yourself and others will feel the belief too.

A Team of Robots or a Team of Leaders?

What is a team of robots? A robot team is a team that will say yes or no to everything without thinking for themselves. They expect the leader to come up with all the solutions. The goal here is to empower the team to be self-sufficient, allowing yourself as the leader to be freed up to look at ways to further progress your end goal as a team. Not being stuck in the detail, which can be delegated to the rest of the team, allows you to continue with the bigger picture at hand whilst the rest of the team keeps everything moving.

Empowering people in the team creates leaders. Obviously, the end goal is directed by you. This should not be confused with making a whole team of leaders where no one listens to anyone else. This is not the goal.

A team of robots will see situations happening in front of them and may realise there is something wrong but not do anything about it. No matter what industry you are in, if something is going wrong and no one speaks up about it, how are you going to know? It takes real courage and belief for the individual to speak up. There will be no courage with robots on your team.

Training and Review

The starting point with any team member in feeling highly valued is the review of the training they have received. The biggest mistake a lot of leaders make is that once employees have been trained, they are left to their own accord thereafter, and they are expected know everything after the training session. The successful method of reviewing the training and testing for a month or even continuously is key to keeping people engaged and active. The only challenge this will present for you is making the time to keep it consistent. By brainstorming how you can make time for this with your team, it is possible to find the time you need.

Investing in Talent

The investment you place in your team members creates confidence, as does the value they desire in their job role. This is the beginning of nurturing and creating leaders. It is then easier to place your demands and expectations on team members to be the best they can be. You can flat-out state to them, "You are the leader of this section of the project. You can tell us all what it is we need to do." Nurturing this is key. Communicate with people on your team for an update on progress. You can be an effective leader by implementing this with your team.

When feelings of being ignored by the leader arise, that is when the quality of a team's winning mentality deteriorates. Of course, this does not mean you have to check in with everyone every hour or every day. But keeping the communication going is important. If you are at the head of your team, and you have your deputies underneath you, they can take on some of these meetings and check-ins for you.

Robots do the bare minimum of what is required of them, and the bullets they have created for themselves involve remaining quiet, as that will allow them to continue at the same level of comfort. How do we create leaders? We get them to take the challenge.

Challenging Yourself and Challenging Your Team

Everyone wants a challenge. By reading this book, you are challenging yourself in order to strengthen yourself and discover your true power. How will you consistently keep challenging yourself to be an inspirational leader?

If you are in an environment where you get measured on targets, how are you going to remain motivated? The self-care aspect is highly important, where you are making time for yourself so you can lead your team. However, to remain on top of your game, the challenge you are presenting yourself is key.

The following are examples of targets in three different fields to get your mind into the gear of how you can challenge yourself and your team. Get into the mindset of brainstorming and then sharing with your team. This is the ultimate goal of this exercise.

- **Manager of a Fashion Store**
  To reach my target for the store to become the number 1 in the UK store ranking in the whole company, I can challenge my team to sell extra products to customers. This has to involve a conversation to convince customers that the purchase will be of use to them, not just selling for the sake of it. This in turn will leave a good impression on the customer, as our team informs them of the range of products we have. After further conversation about occasions they are attending, we will present a solution to the customer which will have met their needs beyond expectation. It's a win for the store as a sale is made; a boost of confidence for my team, as they are

becoming solution-oriented with achieving the target; and a win for the customer, who receives excellent suggestions through great service.

- **Sports Team**
  I will challenge my team to run an extra half mile in training at an intense speed over a consistent period of time. This will help them remain sharp on game day, as the whole team will have that edge of fitness over the opposition. The way I will involve them on this journey is informing them from the beginning that this is the challenge we are setting ourselves, and this is how it will make us into champions with an extra edge. I will measure this by monitoring our fitness compared to the opposition team as the game progresses.

- **Sales Team**
  I will challenge my team to conduct extra research on the products they sell. They will share this with each other in a meeting where we can relay back to the team what we have learnt. At the same time, this will reenforce what they have learnt, and others can learn at the same time through listening. The ultimate goal for the team is to hit the sales target as a team. Their individual targets should be easier to meet too with this challenge of expanding their knowledge.

Challenging your team after the initial training and nurturing aspect is what will inspire them to always be that person. Remember, this must be done with confidence. If you find a team member who is not performing to the level you expect, ask that person, "How would you like to perform?" This is a very powerful question, and by saying this out loud, you make a commitment to yourself and create a measure for future success.

In one-to-one conversations with other members of the team, the talking aloud and sharing of desired results really builds encouragement within team members and you, too, as you are only focussing on success as opposed to the potential pitfalls.

Action Step: Goals

List various ways you can challenge yourself with your goals in leading your team.

- How are you going to raise the bar for yourself?
  How are you going to raise the bar with your team?

Accountability and Commitment

Goal-setting with your team is highly effective, as you are involving them on this journey. They all have their own time constraints, and if you find they are not able to hit their targets, this is where you come in and keep nurturing them with regular catch-ups. Some may say this is too time-consuming, but I do not buy this. If you are a highly committed leader, you will make time for this, as you are now leading a future leader and not a robot.

The coaching and development of the team is something that a lot of leaders neglect. Through their own disorganisation, they fail to keep their team coached. This is where you come in. If you have placed demands on your team, and you have not shown them how those demands can be met, then you are setting them up to fail. This is different from holding their hands or mollycoddling them. This is true leadership, where you are imparting your knowledge of how it can be accomplished. If you are having trouble doing this, you need to learn it yourself. By avoiding the situation, you are going to fail yourself and your team.

A more four-dimensional approach I have seen work is asking team members about their personal goals in life. This will be more effective if you have already built a strong foundation in terms of rapport. What benefit does this have? The wider picture here is engaging their mind to be active in achieving. When you have the inspiration and confidence to talk freely about your personal goals, it branches out into every aspect of performance in your career too.

An example of a personal goal one of my previous team members had was to enquire about a psychology course this individual wanted to study outside of work but had been procrastinating about for a long period of time. This was revealed to me in our one-to-one conversation. The action steps to achieve this goal were made in that meeting, and we wrote down when this individual would enquire about the course and where details could be found. I did not give any of the answers. That particular individual came up with the answers and then took the action step of enquiring about the course and gathering all the details on the planned-for date.

Always get your team members to write down the goals they wish to achieve. It is nothing formal. This is their own goal, and it will further reenforce their self-belief in achieving, whether it be inside or outside of work.

Personal Life

Your leadership skills of leading yourself in your personal life is what *Bite Your Bullet* is all about. Leading yourself to reach your goals is highly important and keeps you motivated to want to achieve. In relationships with others—family, friends, romantic partners—how are you going to lead the way? I'm not talking about dominating other people in your life. This is more about how those in the relationship discuss ideas in a responsive manner.

When you find that mentality of creating leaders in the workplace, you will do the same in your personal life. Notice how people around you see you as an inspiration. The confidence you radiate can inspire those in your personal relationships and create a leading mentality in them too. What could be better than seeing people close to you take control of their life all thanks to you leading your own life? The freedom you create within another allows for a healthier relationship between the two of you as well.

Parenting

As a parent, you are a leader. The leading aspect comes in the form of empowering your child to become bulletproof. You cannot force this or make your child think the same way as you do. Parents are quick to get their children to behave a certain way, as they think this is how they should behave. Childhood years are the best years to build a foundation.

We all know by now that it is never too late to change or heal from your past. Children can go through great or terrible times. The foundation that needs to be taught to children is how they are going to be confident from a young age. Encouraging them to speak up is the best way. Saying *shhh* or *be quiet* out in public is not the best way to reenforce this. They will become like this outside of the home and end up being too cooperative with other children or bad adults out there. You must let them have some form of rebelliousness, which will give them that edge to not let anyone walk over them. They need to be able to stand up to a bully and stand up to dangerous adults, such as paedophiles and perverts.

If you are exposing your children to many activities from a young age—such as swimming, karate, scouts, or whatever clubs there are these days—this is the best way for their personalities to become dynamic in the social arena. Children who are highly talented may show a different side of their personality, where they want to craft their talent. They do this by spending a long time in activity and may seem unsociable. This is far from the case.

Your job here is to lead them to flourish. Taking interest in an activity is the best way to assist them. Ask them to explain what they are doing. Ask them more advanced questions of what techniques they are using.

Let's take the example of art. If your children are really into drawing, ask them what they are looking to draw. Ask them how they have captured the shading or colour work with a genuine compliment. Encourage them to talk about it. There are young artists I have known who have amazing paintings, yet they were too shy to post them on Instagram in fear of what other people might think of their artwork. This is a bad way for an individual to think.

All children can be the best at something. They may want to give up, and you cannot force them to do something. But you can use inspirational techniques to allow them to never give up. This is where a stubborn child could feel good about being resilient and not feeling defeated. This mentality needs to be encouraged with regards to talents or potential interests. Shutting them down or shutting them out is definitely the wrong way to go.

Empowering your children with strength of character is something that will assist them in their adult life. Being rebellious or talking back to parents is something that can be nurtured into something great. If you notice they have a bit of fire in them, you have to look at activities that interest them, such as combat sports. If they are somewhat quiet, don't think they are ignoring you or that they don't care about you. Most likely, they are in deep thought about what it is they want to accomplish.

Modern-day parents have to be there as friends to their children. In the early years, of course, some form of discipline needs to be in place, but children will imitate what they see and hear. If you are constantly swearing in front of your children, they will see this as normal. Then, when you get into a conversation with their teacher and find that your children are swearing or being rude, you'll know where this has come from.

The positive attributes of your personality will also be picked up on. If you are leading with confidence in the way you speak to people and the way you speak to strangers, this will in turn give insight to your children as to how the world can work through different interactions. If you teach your kids to be too polite, they may be in danger of being walked over by corrupt persons. Let them become street smart, and be there for them by allowing them to explain what they want to achieve.

Create the foundations of leading in your children from an early age; that will be the greatest gift they will take into adulthood. They will not need any healing from their past, as they will have been surrounded by positive family influences.

Think about yourself. How have you remembered moments from your past? You may enjoy or not enjoy them dependent upon your experience, but one thing is for sure: you do remember what happened in your childhood when you reflect on moments that happened. The understanding we get as we grow older unlocks some answers from our childhood. Some are pleasant and some not so pleasant. Encourage the strengthening of the mind in your children so they will be able to survive anything in their adult life.

Conclusion

Everyone possesses a level of expertise in some aspect of life. What is it you are knowledgeable in, and how can you communicate this with other people? That is in essence the starting point of realising you are a leader. You will be surprised how easily this transfers into other areas of your life: leading yourself to be able to lead others.

Leading from a place of authenticity in all walks of life, whether it be personal or professional, is the foundation to which those around you will respond to you in trust. We all have a brand that we project to the world. When we show the world our true authentic brand by remaining in our power, this inspires others to follow and, more importantly, creates a belief that they themselves can lead too.

Ultimately, spreading this power to others is the most rewarding feeling you can find. You are improving the lives of others by encouraging them to be the best version of themselves through confidence-building and self-belief—and, more importantly, unlocking the freedom they possess in life.

CHAPTER 12

Mental Fitness: Recharging Oneself

The best superpower I possess in a thought-stimulated world is to step back and recharge my mind's eye.

Since the beginning of this book, my main aim has been to free your mind from imaginary bullets you have created. I want to help you work on yourself to be a better version of who you are by clearing your past pain, organising your week to incorporate your goals, and being a leader of your life and teams or social groups. All this is very enjoyable.

How about the time you need for yourself, to simply recharge? *Bite Your Bullet* is about becoming bulletproof. Even a super-car such as a Ferrari will need TLC, whether it means a car wash and a polish or an engine tune-up through servicing. We are the same. Allow your mind and body to rest when required. The more I begin to write about this chapter, the clearer it becomes to me how vital this is. To become bulletproof is one thing. To remain bulletproof is another. How can we recharge?

Taking into account the levels you have gone through to consistently become the best you can be—and taking on new projects, whether it be with goals you have set or anything else that requires a new version of yourself—ironically, you can become lost again. I remind us all of the earlier stories regarding people who overworked themselves and died. These people at one point or another had goals. They began to achieve their goals, and they did a great job. But where was the recharge for themselves? These people have left behind a big gift for us, clearly showing that we are all important and reminding us always to put ourselves as a priority living a meaningful life.

How can we recharge ourselves? There are many tools out there to help, including meditation, yoga, therapy groups, gardening, playing video games, writing down what you are grateful for, and switching the phone into airplane mode. I have listed some physical activities for all age groups. The one that is most important for me is putting the phone in airplane mode. This is highly important for disciplining ourselves.

Switching Off from the Digital World

Social media can be fun, but it is highly addictive. Work and social groups have been created to speedily send information among members. This is great for when you are at work or staying in touch with friends and family. But the constant pinging or checking your phone for the latest information regarding work communication can become exhausting. Even friendship groups can take a lot out of you.

I have just gone through my phone and realised I have twenty groups, six of which are non-friend groups. It is great to stay in touch and can be really entertaining. I know we have the mute function on our groups. But sometimes a switch-off and individual conversations is what is needed to relax our minds.

When on annual leave from work, I made a point to leave the work social media groups. This disciplined me not to check my phone for any communications. It is tempting to check even if you are on holiday. Ask yourself, if you are having to interact with your professional side, are you doing that from a place of fear?

Then there is Facebook, Snapchat, Instagram, Viber, and loads more that I have not mentioned. How much time do you think you spend on your smartphone using social media when you have nothing to do? There is a measure on smartphones now that inform you how much time you have spent on your phone and a breakdown of social media time itself.

Being Bored Activates Creativity

In today's age, we have lost the art of being bored. I very rarely hear people use the word *bored*. There is always something available to distract us, whether it be smartphones, TV, internet, Netflix, etc. Switching off from everyone around you in your free time is a healthy habit worth establishing.

When I was growing up, before the technology boom, there were only four TV channels and no smartphones. Our only option was to expand our imagination and play with friends or family members outside in the garden or at the park. We would spend time drawing, painting, playing board games, practicing football skills, learning musical instruments, and so on.

It is believed that Edison, inventor of the lightbulb, made 10,000 attempts in all before getting it right. Can you imagine if Edison had a smartphone and social media pinging away on his phone? We can only imagine Edison having a group on his phone with his inventor friends where he would post videos and images of the progress he has made or get distracted by incoming messages. The point is that the fewer distractions we have, the more we can focus and channel our creative powers in achieving a desired result.

A study from the US National Library of Medicine analysed the impact of mobile phone usage. This passage from the abstract highlights the impact phone notifications can have on our productivity:

> Mobile phones generate auditory or tactile notifications to alert users of incoming calls and messages. Although these notifications are generally short in duration, they can prompt task-irrelevant thoughts, or mind wandering, which has been shown to damage task performance. We found that cellular phone notifications alone significantly disrupted performance on an attention-demanding task, even when participants did not directly interact with a mobile device during the task. (https://www.ncbi.nlm.nih.gov/pubmed/26121498/)

Spending that time with yourself and generating ideas and plans is an investment worth making. The best investment is the one we make in ourselves. Even better is to enjoy your free time without wanting to think of plans or goals. Enjoy having time to do nothing.

Mental Fitness

Mental fitness is a term I have used to replace *mental health*. This is my opinion and each to their own, but I feel that *mental health* has a negative connotation. I state this because mental health is always surrounded by discussion of depression and anxiety, and it seems to be more reactive, focused on discovering the problem in an individual rather than taking preventative steps to identify and deal with what is taking place in a person's mind.

Mental fitness is something we can all benefit from, just as we benefit from lifting weights in the gym for our physical fitness. Both make everyday tasks that much easier, as we have greater strength. Physically, we are prepared for everyday tasks such as lifting groceries or running for a bus; we find this easy due to our physical conditioning. The same can be applied to mental fitness. Making time for ourselves, encouraging our mind to develop ideas, and writing down anything that is bothering us is a form of a working out.

The habit many of us have fallen into when we come home from school or work is to fall into a comfort zone of switching on the TV, eating anything we see as a quick fix, and doing this for the next few hours. Or should I say, we go to our phone and scroll through random social media feeds that do not feed our minds.

Your mind is bombarded by information throughout the day. You walk down the street, and you see advertisements on billboards. You sit at a bus stop, and there's another advert. You scroll through your smartphone, and adverts pop up or show on the side of the page you are looking at. Other adverts now appear in video clips we view on social media. Then, if you are travelling on the tube, there are more adverts.

You get notifications on your phone from social media groups, emails at work, personal email notifications on your smartphone. If you have to collect groceries on the way home, this is another list to remember. I can go on and on. Our minds are stimulated with all this information nearly every minute of the day, and we are required to react and think all the time.

When is your mind at rest for your thoughts to run free? The action steps in this book have all been tools for increasing your mental fitness. We are allowing our brains to switch off from the information overload and become stronger through self-care.

Action Step: Switching Off

Consider the following points for yourself:

1. When you have a day off from work or school, do you switch it off completely and not think about that side of your of life?
2. Do you mute your work social media groups?
3. Do you get calls or texts from your work colleagues on your day off?
4. When you are on annual leave from work, do you leave work WhatsApp groups?
5. When you are on annual leave, do you get calls and texts from colleagues?
6. When your friends want to do something and want you to get involved, and you do not want to, do you make it clear that you have other things to do, or do you go with the crowd?

I am sure there are additional questions you can think of for yourself. Brainstorm how you are on your own time. Do you get disturbed or interrupted in the time you have for yourself?

Having read the chapters so far, especially on confidence-building and remaining in your power, you should be on track to speak up to any of the above questions and set your own healthy boundaries. This can apply to not only work situations but also personal situations as well. Take a check of your own boundaries at present. You are powerful enough to set and put these boundaries in place with everyone you know. You are bulletproof now.

Mental fitness should be considered as a means of being prepared for any situation you may face. When the time comes that there are a lot of demands placed on you, requiring a lot of your time and energy, you will be prepared for the situation at hand. It will not make you feel overwhelmed. Whether the situation is an argument or an emergency, you'll have control of your mind and be able to act appropriately. Managing your mind through mental fitness means knowing how and when to act.

Anxiety and Depression

There is a need to highlight these, as mental health, as it is commonly known in society, focusses on these two feelings. Cases of anxiety and depression have increased and have become more common in the teenage years. When I was a teenager, I did not know of any friends or people my age who were anxious or depressed. Obviously, it was not talked about so much as it is now. We had carers in our school who were available for counselling sessions should anyone require it, but one thing I am sure of is that not many kids my age at the time were on antidepressants.

The doctors who are prescribing antidepressants these days are not helping people to build their minds to be bulletproof. Issuing pills is a quick fix and does not address the problem at hand. Of course, it is great as a temporary measure. I encourage you all to make time for yourself to be able to keep from slipping into anxiety or depression.

My observation is that the more our minds are stimulated through our daily activities and routines, the higher the probability of slipping into anxiety will be. A million thoughts are racing through our heads, and we may not be able to switch them off to recharge our minds and get a healthy amount of sleep. We may lie awake with such anxious thoughts about the future as the following:

- What do I need to do next?
- I need to do this.
- I don't have the time.
- What food shall I give my child tonight?
- What shall I eat?

This can occur in any age group. Many people I know between the ages of 20 and 55 have these thoughts racing through their head every day. Don't let your work life take over your mind and life in general. We have the power to adapt to this. Mental fitness is all about adapting to everyday life and feeling in control of yourself—not being under the control of others, but yourself. The only thing you can control in life is yourself. By taking a step back and decluttering your mind, you will find that you have the headspace to be ready for your day.

Remember confidence-building and energy management. These are all tools we possess in our mind's gym. I promise you, with a definitive purpose for your life and the methods I've shown you to build yourself up, you can inspire those around you to adapt to all situations in your life and thus prevent any anxious feelings.

How to Cope with Depression

I know we all experience loss and disappointment at some stage in our life. It is a part of life. The mental fitness approach to keeping us from spiralling out of control will keep us from slipping too deep into depressive states. I am confident that all people can drag themselves out of depression. I use the word *drag* on purpose, as it is a heavy feeling we can all have when we have experienced a big loss. There is no sugar-coating it.

How to cope? We know the answer already: mental fitness. This will prepare us to respond to all situations. We have the tool now of clearing, which involves going through the pain and spitting the pain out. This all helps.

I know people who have let their bullet haunt them for many years until they cleared these feelings from themselves. I too have been there when experiencing loss. I have dragged myself out of those moments of disappointment, as when we are in that state, it seems like there is no point in living anymore. But as a standing-strong person, to inspire everyone who reads this, I can honestly state we have the superpowers of feeling new and improved again as long as we confront and go through these dark times with the aid of the tools I have used in this book.

Leaders will experience the same fate as everyone in terms of personal loss or disappointments in life, but the leading mind of inspiration will always find a way out of everything. This is the superpower we develop, which results in the ultimate bulletproof mind and an awareness that we are responsible for ourselves and the environment around us.

Take the example of single parents. People become single parents for a variety of reasons—a loss from death of their partner, a separation from falling out of love, cheating, etc. These are all painful events to experience, but the single parent is the leader of the family. Whether it is looking after one child or looking after four children, that right there is an example of a leader facing difficult times.

Other leaders can be your manager at work or a director. Those people will also experience loss, but how they lead themselves through those situations is what will motivate them to get out of those situations of low feelings. Having that motivation to lead is what can drag a person out of these situations. Remember, we are all leaders of ourselves. If you are feeling down and out, lead yourself out of it. The help of everyone around you can pull you out of depression, but only when you are ready to lead yourself out.

Many people I have known throughout the years have taken antidepressants prescribed by their GP. All have informed me of the effect it has on them, which is that they don't feel themselves, and their feelings have been numbed. Before any tablets were present in society, how do you think people coped with feeling low or depressed? Sure, there were people who turned to alcohol and drugs, but that is a small portion of society. Everyone had to make it out of there somehow. People had no choice but to be tough. They had to bite their bullet regardless of the situation.

Tablets can mask the pain and allow you to avoid the healing of emotional wounds within you. Confronting is a better option. An affirmation to always remind yourself of is: "The best superpower I possess in a thought-stimulated world is to step back and recharge my mind's eye."

Mind's Eye

What is the mind's eye, you ask? The mind's eye is not something far out there. Of course, those familiar with meditation know there is a third eye, but for the sake of this book, we are concentrating on the mental element of life, in which there is a mind's eye.

Our eyes see the world. Our mind understands the world. When we speak of the bullet always following us around everywhere until bitten, that is our mind's eye creating these limitations we place on ourselves. Stepping back and recharging the mind's eye gives us clarity on what we need to do next.

Remember that you truly see with your mind when you understand the world around you. Use the superpower of stepping back, and your mind's eye will be clear and present.

Conclusion

To summarise the importance of remaining on top of our goals, the recharge aspect is what will always keep us sharp. I am sure Elvis Presley wanted to remain sharp and achieve more goals he may have had on top of what he had already accomplished. You have to remember Elvis was living off many tablets to assist him in feeling awake and separate tablets to get him to sleep. The step-back opportunity was not there for him, as he was always living off everyone else's time. Take his life as a blessing to us all, not just in his career but to learn that we must make time for our mind to look after our life in general.

Kanye West, Lady Gaga, Rita Ora, and Selena Gomez, to name a few celebrities, have all felt exhaustion and have ended up in hospital to rejuvenate. We are just as important as celebrities, and exhaustion in the non-celebrity world is just as real for a single parent looking after more than one child or a parent supporting a family by trying to please those in both their home life and work life. Teenagers may place pressure on themselves in wanting to achieve the best grades possible and stressing out over exams and social pressures.

Microsoft founder Bill Gates makes an important investment in himself each year. It has become known to the public that he takes a "think week." I am sure there are many people in the world who do something similar. But I'm using Bill Gates here as an inspirational example. During his think week, he switches off from his work and technology in general.

As all of us on this *Bite Your Bullet* journey are growing stronger, we can incorporate and adapt something similar into our own lives. If Bill Gates, one of the most successful entrepreneurs of our time, can place this much investment in himself, we can and should too. We are human, just like Bill. Remember, you have such a high value in what you have to offer that you deserve the best self-care treatment too.

Mental fitness keeps any future bullets from forming. I cannot emphasise enough that if you have taken the time to build confidence in yourself with self-belief, you will find it even more important to recharge in order to rebuild and excel. The biggest favour you can do to yourself and the world in general is to recharge in order to present your best self to the world.

CHAPTER 13

Physical Fitness: Bulletproofing Mind and Body

There is a perception that the mind and body are separate. From my years of building a bulletproof mind, I can tell you that the physical aspect of the body goes in sync with the mind and is just as important in keeping it sharp. Everyone has different fitness levels and abilities. There are people who are in wheelchairs but have good physical conditioning, as they still work out and are very strong when they have dedicated themselves to building upper-body strength.

What we all have in common is the choice we have to move our bodies—whether it be through sport, gym, walking in the park, climbing, cycling, gardening, etc. Making an attempt at moving the body through pushing our physical levels is important in assisting our mind.

It is common knowledge that activity increases oxygen levels in the brain, allowing for extra neurons to be formed, but that is the science. Here we highlight the power you feel when you are developing your body—and the feel-good factor afterwards. It's not just the endorphins being produced after a workout but also the sense of accomplishment you feel that you are progressing your body and treating it with respect. The following advice should be taken into consideration with a doctor's guidance if you have any health issues, as my guide to fitness involves pushing ourselves to our limits.

It is understandable that people need someone to motivate them. However, through the journey of *Bite Your Bullet*, you are inspiring yourself, which fuels your motivation. You are now at a point where you know how to plan your week and incorporate goals. There are no excuses.

Society is very flexible and forgiving these days. We are all encouraged to take it slow and wait until we're ready. To go slightly off topic, as an analogy, I remember back in the day playing computer games. You could only move forward; you could not go backwards. Take Super Mario, for example, where you would go through the level and have a certain number of lives. Once those lives were gone, you were dead (in the game) and had to start all over again, no matter how far you had gotten. The computer games we have now give us infinite chances to advance forward. We are challenged, but not to the same extent as with the old games, where it was do or die.

My point in bringing this up is that we have to get ourselves out of that zone of comfort we are coddled with these days. With the physical fitness part, let's take it in our stride, really have no excuses, and do it.

The following daily exercises are presented as a useful guide. I have avoided using too much gym jargon to keep it accessible for all, not just people who have an athletic side. As this is not a gym book, I have outlined the basic exercises below. Further information can be found online if you are looking to measure yourself against certain standards. For example, the maximum push-up limits can be found online, where it measures whether you are average, below, or above the certain number of reps you can perform.

Cardio Training

The Bleep Test (Multi-Stage Fitness Test)

For those not familiar with this test, it is where you do shuttle runs back and forth along a distance of 20 metres. There is a line at either end of the 20 metres, and you run back and forth in timing with a bleeping sound that is made. You have to run to the line and reach it before the bleep sounds. After every minute, the speed at which the bleep sounds becomes quicker. There are 18 to 21 levels, and for the extremely fit amongst us, you would be sprinting back and forth until you run out of breath and have to stop, or you do not reach the line in time for the bleep.

This can be done at any fitness level. What I like about this test is that it pushes you to your extreme limit of cardio. If you have access to 20 metres of space, definitely give this a go. YouTube has the test available too. You can run this with a pair of headphones for the timing of the bleep. If you do not have access to this test, that is no problem.

Interval Training

There is another running technique called *interval training*. This type of training consists of high intense running to low intense running. This is accessible for all, as we can do this running around our area on the pavement or park. Two good measures I have used are street lights or trees. As you are jogging, you can sprint your fastest between two street lights or trees, and then slow down your running again.

Raising your heart rate and lowering it randomly with interval training is the best way to strengthen the cardiac muscle in your heart and the overall breath flow in your lungs, as opposed to running at a constant speed. Running at a constant speed becomes comfortable and is all about conditioning you to run over a long distance. The cardiac system does not become challenged.

The feeling one has after interval training is very rewarding. You have taken your body to its limit of high intense running and made yourself uncomfortable through breathing really heavily and wanting to give up, but you didn't. I find after doing this kind of running, I can breathe much easier, and the breath flows out very smoothly. The extra blood sent to the rest of my body allows me to move with ease.

How does this link with the mind? This is key to the bulletproof strengthening of the mind, as we are taking ourselves to places we have not been before. We are going to an uncomfortable zone with our body, and we are pushing ourselves. The effect this has on our mind is one of being present in the moment, as you feel you are surviving this intense running, and you forget about anything else in your life. It is just you and the breathing.

Bringing yourself into this survival mode of breathing intensely can make you feel alive and rejuvenated. Bringing yourself to the present moment is what allows you to feel alive and free. As mentioned earlier, the thoughts of what could happen in the future are anxious thoughts and can put you in a place of worry and despair. Running intensely frees you of all this.

Do this for yourself, and if you know people with anxiety, inspire them to follow suit with you. Do this consistently four times a week for two weeks, and you will notice the difference in your fitness level and your overall peace of mind. You will begin to get through situations with extra clarity.

Take work as an example. If you have been training outside of work with this intense running, when you return to work, you will feel your work life is easy. The work world does not require you to push yourself to your extreme limit. Your work life can only push you by placing further stress on you, with extra projects or workload. If you can survive your own intense running, work life will feel like nothing in comparison. This, I promise, will be the case once tried and tested by everyone reading this.

Daily Push-Ups

Push-ups strengthen your upper body, chest, arms, and lats. I would encourage fifty push-ups to begin with. I do not mean fifty push-ups non-stop. Break it up a bit. Start with ten push-ups in a row. Rest for a few minutes, then do another ten. Repeat until in total you have done fifty. For those who feel they are at a better fitness level, go for a hundred push-ups in total.

The challenge to test yourself is to perform your maximum number of push-ups in a row. You may find that in your first week, you are able to do ten to fifteen push-ups in a row non-stop. Test yourself twice a week. You will find that the stronger you get, the more push-ups you'll be able to do non-stop.

Why is this important to the mind? Daily push-ups build your strength and endurance. When you approach this for the first time, you may find it difficult. As each set passes by, you will find yourself becoming stronger. Time your rest periods in between going on to the next set. If you have done fifteen push-ups, wait two minutes and go again. If you feel you need a three-minute rest in between, take three, and as you become stronger over the coming weeks, decrease the rest period.

A good measure to note down twice a week is to see how many push-ups you can complete in the space of two minutes. Note this down to track your progress. You may wish to do this on a daily basis the stronger you get.

Ratings For Men (based on age)	20-29	30-39	40-49	50-59	60+
Excellent	> 54	> 44	> 39	> 34	> 29
Good	45-54	35-44	30-39	25-34	20-29
Average	35-34	24-34	20-29	15-24	10-19
Poor	20-34	15-24	12-19	8-14	5-9
Very Poor	< 20	< 15	< 12	< 8	< 5

Ratings For Women (based on age)	20-29	30-39	40-49	50-59	60+
Excellent	> 48	> 39	> 34	> 29	> 19
Good	34-48	25-39	20-34	15-29	5-19
Average	17-33	12-24	8-19	6-14	3-4
Poor	6-16	4-11	3-7	2-5	1-2
Very Poor	< 6	< 4	< 3	< 2	< 1

http://gameofhealth.com/the-seven-numbers-resources/fitness-test/pushup-test

Sit-Ups

Sit-ups strengthen your abs and back. These are important for your core strength. Core strength in general is important to overall health and will greatly benefit you into old age, as it strengthens you to hold your balance and keep your posture upright.

Try to do a hundred sit-ups per day. By this, I mean blocked out in sets of fifteen to twenty reps. If you are a beginner, you may have to start off with ten reps and aim to do fifty per day. Either way, ten of these is more progress than zero. With sit-ups you may be able to do more. You will eventually get to the level of doing a hundred sit-ups in a row non-stop.

Why is this important to the mind? You feel that you are planning ahead for your future body. How do you want to be in old age? Do you want to be dependent on others, or do you want to remain independent where you can support yourself?

This all links to the mind and your confidence within. You will know you are able to be the best in life through this physical conditioning you are doing now. It doesn't matter if you are approaching old age, there is always time to change and create your path. The famous runner Fauja Singh, who is currently 108 years of age, rediscovered running at the age of 89. He holds many records for running long distances for the category of over 90 years of age.

Squats

Take caution with squats if you have suffered a knee injury. If this is the case, you know your own body's limits as to how low you can go for a squat. If you cannot bend your knees fully all the way, go halfway to begin with. Over time, you may be able to strengthen and push the mobility of your squat to become more flexible. It's best to perform this after you have got your body warm through your cardio, as your joints will be more loose and supple, allowing you extra range of motion around the knee joint.

Squats are great for us all, as the lower body is the foundation of the upper body. Having strong legs allows you to feel mobile and fluid when performing daily activities, such as walking upstairs or running for a bus. If you are doing this in sync with the cardio training, you will find that your running will become much easier as the weeks go by. There will be that extra spring in your step when walking and running as your leg muscles become more powerful.

If you are unable to perform squats. then get a chair and sit down and stand up on the chair, beginning with twenty reps. This is also an exercise to measure ageing and elderly people's strength of how many reps they are able to perform.

Bonus Task: Cold Shower

There have been many mentions recently of cold showers for good health. Apparently, they can boost your immune system and keep you alert. Cold showers are good for your muscles in terms of blood flow. Before beginning this, if you have any underlying health conditions, please be careful in case of fainting or if you have a heart condition.

This method I am going to outline is something I credit to Wim Hof, as he is someone who is an advocate for the cold as a way to control the immune system. My reasons for cold showers has nothing to do with health, as the research I have conducted does not state whether it is fact that it can boost your immune system and have other health benefits. There are even cases mentioned of how it has assisted people with depression/anxiety. One person pointed out that when they were in the navy, they never felt depressed and were always challenged. When they were out of the navy and in civilian life, they felt depressed—that is, until they started taking cold showers. The reasoning here had more to do with how the discomfort of the cold made this individual feel challenged again.

This was an interesting aspect that captured my attention. I myself have been taking cold showers daily after downloading the thirty-day challenge from Wim Hof's app. His advocacy was for a stronger immune system. This may be true, and he has proved it with his accomplishments in the freezing cold; scientific experiments have been conducted upon him. If this is a by-product of exposing yourself to cold temperatures, that is great. However, for the sake of challenging ourselves mentally, I believe that putting ourselves in an uncomfortable environment by choice assists in developing a mindset of being ready for anything.

To follow the Wim Hof method, start with warm water and gradually decrease the temperature or increase the amount of cold water. The target for your first day should be ten to fifteen seconds of cold water. As the days go by, you can begin to extend the time. Once you reach one minute, you will be surprised at how far you have come from not being able to previously withstand ten seconds.

This, I believe, is a great tool to foster a *Bite Your Bullet* mindset, as you are putting yourself in the cold temperature by choice. The only person you are affecting is yourself, and you gain confidence for going through any other uncomfortable situations that can potentially arise in life. Nervous about public speaking? Job interviews? The cold shower will give you a feeling of power that you have just undergone something uncomfortable and you are fine.

Punchbag: Unleashing the Warrior Within

As mentioned in the chapter on confidence, if you have a punchbag, then great. If you don't, then punch a pillow or use the one at your gym, if they have one. The purpose of this exercise is to remain in touch with the aggression within you. As mentioned earlier with not shying away from violence in terms of understanding, this is exactly it. If you join a boxing club, they have it for all levels of ability.

The confidence you gain within from striking an opponent or a punchbag allows you to express your fighting technique and style so you become more familiar with another part of yourself. This can be done as shadow punching and kicking, but having an impact at the other end is highly effective, as you can feel how hard your punching and kicking travels.

The whole point of the following exercises is for you to become comfortable with striking with both your hands and feet. This is highly important to allow your brain to register what form you are used to if you ever have to self-defend in a real situation. The impact felt at the end of the punchbag will allow you to get used to striking with intent. You must turn into an almost beastlike person when you are going all out with the exercises below. Tapping into these areas of yourself allows you to express who you are. The more you know about yourself, the better you will feel.

Set yourself a time of fifteen minutes to complete both exercises. It is important to remain decisive with this time limit and to complete as many as you can within this set time. If you wish to go on longer, you must repeat the whole process in that specified time limit.

Exercise 1

Punch the punchbag repetitively as fast as you can with both hands alternating. This will test your stamina and strike force. Start off with thirty seconds of light power punches followed by one minute of rest. Then thirty seconds of medium power punches followed by one minute of rest. Then finally thirty seconds of maximum power punches followed by two minutes of rest. Then repeat the whole cycle from the beginning. The key in this is to punch as fast as you can so you are pushing yourself.

If you are an extreme beginner, halve the time. Do fifteen seconds instead of thirty. If you feel you are at an advanced level, then increase to forty-five seconds if you can. Thirty seconds is an acceptable time for most, and this will be tiring.

Exercise 2

Kick the punchbag with a roundhouse kick. If you are not sure how a roundhouse kick is performed, you can find videos online. It is easy for anyone to perform. With this one, it will be the quantity you measure yourself, timed with a stopwatch, of how many you can perform in a set amount of time.

Start off with ten roundhouse kicks with your right leg and then ten with your left leg. Time yourself with a stopwatch to see how long it takes to complete these. Over time, as you become more conditioned, you can increase the quantity of kicks or keep it at ten kicks and see how fast you progress every time you test yourself.

Use the same system as the punching, where you can go from light, medium, to maximum power in your kicks. For the advanced level, increase your count to thirty kicks. Speed is also important in this one, and your stamina is tested.

If you feel you would like to attend boxing, MMA, or karate classes to experience facing an opponent or just to be with like-minded individuals, then by all means go and get involved. You will feel a sense of value in yourself.

Conclusion

The by-product of all the above will be your body shaping up. The appearance is not the goal here. It is the way we feel when we are becoming strong both mentally and physically. But hey, if you see that your abs are starting to shape up through sit-ups, your shoulders and chest through push-ups, and your thighs and butt through squats, then that's an extra boost to you, because you have created that aesthetic result yourself.

What this does to your mind is allow you to feel the progress not just in your muscles but in your confidence too. The reenforcement of all the tools gathered in the earlier chapters and incorporating this with the physical is what will make you feel not only bulletproof in the mind but in the body also, where you are willing to take on anything. The body is simply an extension of the mind, and a powerful mind can extend to reflecting a powerful body.

A lot of people do not realise that once they have strengthened their mind and mental powers, there is another level that is created when they strengthen the body too. You simply don't know until you know. This is the beauty in self-discovery—that the journey of self-development never ends.

Once you feel you have mastered the basic physical exercises outlined above, you naturally may feel like you want to perform more advanced exercises or study more nutrition/fitness from books or the web. You may get so into that you want to invest in a personal trainer.

Referring back to the effect this has on daily life, the best and most recent example I can give you is regarding my own life at present. I have targeted myself to run 2.08 miles in fifteen minutes. Whilst I have not reached that goal (15 minutes and 13 seconds is my PB), the effects within have been incredible. I was not expecting myself to feel so powerful in my lungs and circularity system. Simple daily activities such as walking, going up the stairs at work, and lifting objects have become more enjoyable. Even when driving the car, when sitting there for extended periods of time if travelling long distances, my commute feels different, as I am more flexible in my body. I do not feel I have a stiff body when sitting in that same position.

These small differences have a major impact on daily living. I strongly encourage all readers to reap the rewards of the basic exercises outlined above. Feel the difference in your daily lives. You literally will feel superhuman.

Think of self-care as a tree. The healthier the tree, the better fruit it can offer.

CHAPTER 14

Icing on the Cake: The Winning Mentality

The winning mentality is how we should think and feel every day. That hashtag *#Winning* is used when a person is having that winning feeling within and wishes to express it. To me, it is a state of flow and acceptance of wanting to be a winner.

The determination to win is the starting point. This goes with everything. If you are finding yourself unmotivated to do small jobs, you are not on the winning path. A small job might be printing a document, but you don't want to because you have to open up your laptop, find the document from your email, copy it onto your word processor, then get your printer connected and print it. The process I have just described sounds a bit exaggerated, but it's not. I have been there myself in the past where I have had to take these steps. As it is such a tedious task for something so simple, it is easy to brush it under the carpet and say, "I'll do it tomorrow."

If you find yourself not wanting to do something when you should be doing it, correct yourself immediately and change yourself within to remind yourself about the winning mentality. Any task that has to be completed in any aspect of your life—gardening, washing your car, hoovering, filing your documents—do them all with efficiency and vigour. This is the winning mentality in action.

Challenge yourself if you must by seeing how fast you can accomplish these tasks against the clock. When you are at your workplace, do the same thing with intensity and vigour. Don't get caught up with your colleagues slowing you down or members of your team doing this if you are running your business. This intensity and vigour to want to be the best at what you are doing is what will keep you on the path of success. You will find the efficiency aspect will make you more determined to fill your other time with ways to expand your knowledge.

I mentioned at work not to get distracted by colleagues. Obviously, you have to find a balance of wanting to get on with your peers, but as a boss, colleague, or business owner, you have to set the pace. Even if others make a comment on your speed, it is because they are feeling intimidated by your commitment. Most bosses will be pleased with your efforts. Making yourself a victim of "why should I be the only one doing this whilst everyone is working slow or lazily" is not the way to keep a winning attitude. I promise you, you will find that the more you are committed to your actions with intensity and vigour, the more you will automatically want to progress in all areas of your life.

When friends and family question what you are getting up to, whether it be a painting you are doing or DIY on your house, be strong enough to hold that winning mentality of you on your mission accomplishing what needs to be done. Am I saying to be stubborn with your winning mentality? Yes, but in a way of self-love and not competition to just be right over someone else. If there is something you are doing which you really want to accomplish, then you go for it, my friend.

Be realistic. Analyse yourself, as we have covered before. Have you really got the knowledge and talent to fulfil something? Only then should you remain stubborn with winning. Let's rephrase that to remaining focussed with winning: if you are not a boss in your workplace, set the pace of completing tasks. You'll find that you will become motivated to accomplish bigger goals. Hobbies can also be enjoyable with intense focus as opposed to taking up a hobby for a few weeks and letting it fizzle out.

Motivational Moments to Spark You Back Up

Failure and setbacks are only temporary. If you find yourself not reaching the desired outcome, you have to find the right approach.

I remember there was one moment when I felt like I failed at something. I was laying down on the ground looking up at the ceiling. I accepted defeat. Then, straight away, through the years of conditioning I had placed on myself, a voice within immediately would not let me feel defeated. It's like a GPS system inside which is only directed towards success and winning. Immediately, I became almost angry at myself for having a thought like that. It spurred me on to push forward and get up off the ground.

No matter how far off the route you may go, you will always have a fire within you which will light up and fan the flames of winning. If you ever find yourself becoming demotivated in any aspect of your life, go into the silence temporarily and accept the perceived defeat. See if you can get back up. I know I can, and I know many of you can too. Your journey into winning and being bulletproof is too strong for you to ever be deterred. Test your inner spark with this.

Speaking About It

The more you talk about winning, the more winning you will experience. If you want to see a red car in the street, you will be looking for it more often than not, and you will begin to notice more red cars. When you are researching a product you want to buy, do you ever start seeing more adverts or shops that are the same as you are looking for? These are all nudges steering you in the right direction.

Speak about winning as much as you like—with the right people, of course. These are people who are happy for your success or looking to win themselves at something they want to do. The energy you feel should be a feeling of lightness that you can take on anything and everything you want to do. This is how you will know you are on the winning path.

Universe and Winning

There is a metaphysical space in my experience of attracting winning. Some may call it the law of attraction. If you are an atheist and have no belief in metaphysical attributes, you have to take a moment to take stock of your own life and connect the dots of how situations have come to fruition. The spaces between the air and ourselves are all vibrational particles. When on a winning or losing streak, you are tuning in to that vibration from the vibration you emit from your own body.

Think of a radio channel. There is a radio signal broadcast from the station. If it is classical, rap, pop—all of these have an audience. All those who tune in to their preferred music have matched the radio frequency, and they are in sync with this. If classical music fans had no interest in rap music and attempted to rap with the artist, they would not feel in sync. And vice versa—if rappers wanted to listen to calming classical music, they might feel frustrated by the slowness. (By the way, this is just an example; there are fans of rap who listen to classical and vice versa.)

We are a product of Earth. Our planet is 70 per cent water, and our body is 70 per cent water. We have the air through which we breathe, and Earth has wind. We have the fire within electrical sparks in our brains and throughout our body, and Earth has its electrical pulses it can produce—lightning, for example. Our body knows how to defend itself and transport minerals around different body parts. Earth can do the same.

Sands from the Sahara Desert have been found on cars in London. The planet transported them from the Sahara all the way to the Amazon rainforest to provide nutrients for the Amazon. That is how in sync planet Earth is with itself, and our bodies can be in sync also. There are more similarities I can mention. The last and main one is Earth's magnetic field, which protects life on Earth and itself and what it can attract. Earth only lets the correct things enter its atmosphere which are meant for this planet.

Our bodies have the same power. Each of us has an electromagnetic field we emit to everyone depending on how we are feeling. The feeling of winning is something we tune into and magnify. With all the steps taken throughout *Bite Your Bullet*, we are shaping ourselves for winning constantly.

Respecting ourselves and placing the highest value on what we want is the powerful vibration we send out to the universe, and in turn we tune into that radio frequency of winning. There is an unlimited amount for everyone. Everyone can win if they choose to do so. Competing over another is not the energy you want to win by, as it will place you in a state of fear—a fear of losing. This frequency will only direct you to struggle.

Any moment you begin to feel defeated in any way, you will not allow yourself to have these feelings, as you are already in tune with the universal energy and the law of winning. The law of winning is the same as a Japanese proverb: "Fall down 7 times, stand up 8." Simple and effective. I love that quote, as the resilience you feel just from reading that is what the *Bite Your Bullet* mentality is all about. The bulletproof mind for winning is where you want to be. Create that frequency and emit it to the universe. Life will be a breeze.

Action Step: Tools and Techniques

Giving yourself visual cues throughout your day is enough to remind you who you want to be. There are many methods out there. Here are some to try.

Vision Board

A vision board is where you place images of what you desire. It can be a picture of a sports car you want or a picture of a heavy dumbbell weight that you want to lift. It could be starting your own business with a picture of an office with your own company's name made into the logo. You can add anything you want to your vision board—mostly of success and what you want.

Vision boards to keep you on track can consist of images such as a first-place trophy or a first-place medal, as well as positive affirmations such as "I am the best" and "I am winning"—anything motivational you can think of. The key to this is placing it in a prominent location that you will look at many times. Look at it first thing when you wake up and last thing before you go to bed, for example. You can have a mini one that you take around with you in your bag. Visual cues throughout the day are important for remaining consistent. Disturbances throughout the day can make you push your successes to the back of your mind.

Visualising through Meditation

You don't have to become a mystic or a yogi to begin meditation. The type of meditation we are speaking of here is visualising your success and winning. You hold an image in your mind of success and winning. See yourself smiling, happy, and dressed according to how you would like to be living, if that is part of your goal. See yourself accomplishing. Imagine how you are feeling during these moments. The mind will transmit this feeling, and you will know what winning feels like all through yourself. You do not need to seek it, as you will become the winning feeling. This is where you want to be throughout the day. Remember, the feeling transmits the vibration.

Shouting "Win" Whilst Fist-Clenching

This technique is effective when you have accomplished something and you clench your fist in silence. This is how it goes.

We are going to use the word *winning* for the example. You can use the word *winning* or *come ON*, which fires some people up with energy and motivation. Choose a word that will ignite your passion, but the word *winning* is effective if you have no other word, and the present-tense verb will immediately place you in the present moment and be a call to action.

Stand in a safe space where you feel comfortable. At home is a good place. Shout "Winning!" whilst clenching your fist real tight, and you can put your whole body into it. What I mean by this is you can punch forward if you like while shouting "*Winning!*" Or you can step forward and clench your fist and shout it. Other methods I have seen people use are acting like you have just won in sports and going to the ground on your knees celebrating like sports players do. Either way, follow these steps:

1. Shout loud and say "*Winning!*" Elongate the shout as you want to cherish this moment with all your feeling behind it. You should feel your face have that passion and eyes fill with energy of determination.
2. The shouting of "*Winning*" on this one does not have to last long. And you perform the same movement, but it's important to clench the fist real tight.
3. This time, you don't do the body movements. You just clench your fist (still tightly) and assertively saying "Winning!"
4. Clench your fist tightly and say "Winning" more quietly.
5. Clench your fist tightly and whisper "Winning!"
6. Clench your fist tightly and say nothing.

What you should find is that when you succeed at something, you will automatically clench your fist, as you will recognise the winning feeling you have. If you are about to take on a task, test, or exam, and you want to attack it with a winning mentality, just clench your fist tightly a few times whilst saying *Win* in your head, or whisper it to yourself if it naturally comes out. Hey, if you want to shout it in front of people, then do what you feel is best for you.

The important aspect of this is to clench your fist tightly whenever you do this. The passion is channelled into the fist you make, and this is how it is physically expressed through you, thus creating the winning feeling throughout your mind and body. I have found myself clenching my fist tight when completing something that required my focus.

Small Notes

Other reminders you can have for yourself are small notes in your wallet or bag stating an affirmation of winning or what you want to become or do to keep you on track. The following are some examples:

- Winning!
- I am eating fresh fruit and veg.
- I am succeeding in everything I do.
- I have won my goals.
- I am the best.

These must be referred to throughout the day. Habitually sticking to this will ultimately test how committed and serious you are about your actions with creating winning habits. If you find yourself phasing out after a week or two, the question I would throw at you is, how bad do you want it? How much do you really want to win in your life?

All of the above techniques are tools for you to utilise to motivate others who may be inspired by you. It does not mean you have to do all of them. It is entirely up to you. You may want to vary these over the course of weeks, months, or years. Shape your mindset into the winning mentality by taking action always. That is why the above techniques are tangible winning habits to create.

Conclusion

This is the beginning of your journey into a new level of trust and faith in yourself. I have stated there is an energy in the universe we tune into. All the elements in the previous chapters are there to shape you into a strong, bulletproof mind, which in turn tunes in to the frequency of the universe where you'll attract only the best into your life. Even the self-defence aspect is reenforcing your trust in yourself that you are a badass, and you'll project that into the world without uttering a word.

I will end this chapter with a very recent example of me in a swimming pool which took place over the weekend. I hadn't been swimming for a few years. My cousins have a swimming pool in their garden, and I am lucky to be able to use it. Whilst I got used to the water again, I began to trust the water and became comfortable and felt one with it.

However, on my second visit in the pool, I remembered an action I found difficult when I was a teenager of spinning head over heels in the pool—a somersault underwater. A fear came over me as I attempted this, as I had a weird fear of allowing my head to rotate underwater, where I felt out of control. Through my own learnings from *Bite Your Bullet*, I refused to accept defeat, as this did not allow me to fully enjoy myself in the pool.

That night, I could not perform the underwater somersault. I left my cousins' house disappointed in myself. The third opportunity I got (the weekend just gone), I was determined. The night before, I was visualising how I could spin underwater. I was going through the motions visualising in my head with meditation how I would perform this. Stupid thoughts began to enter my mind of not being able to do it. If this ever happens to you, fight it, conquer it, and mould it to your vision of success. That is only fear speaking. Fear is an illusion.

Moving onto the day I was there in the swimming pool, I was all set. I began to exhale as I went underwater and tried to spin. I was determined as ever. It took me over two hours. Whilst I was talking to my cousins and just swimming around, I was thinking about asking them to help me and informing them of my goal. I decided if I could not do it soon, then I needed assistance.

All of a sudden, I was underwater, and I felt really comfortable. I immediately performed the underwater somersault I wanted to. This was done with no thought, and the action of moving my arms in a rotating motion came to me automatically. This was something I'd never tried before. I felt the winning mentality and feeling of accomplishment. I began to spin underwater many times, forwards and backwards. Now I will never have that fear creep up ever again.

I have done this visualisation technique before. I mention this to celebrate my victory, as it is one to me. Some of you have probably been doing far more advanced swimming manoeuvres for years and see my accomplishment as something easy. But this is the lesson here, which I mentioned near the beginning of our journey: everyone has a win. Winning in all areas of my life and refusing to be defeated is what allowed me to accomplish my goal of the underwater somersault.

Had I not accomplished it that day, I would have been highly disappointed with myself. The next time I would have gone swimming, I would have asked for help—for someone to spot me whilst I did it. I chose to do this alone, as that is how I wanted to accomplish it. If you are not good at something and you want to get better at it, the best thing to do is ask an expert to help you out. I was seriously considering, if I could not perform the underwater spin that day, I was going to enrol in swimming classes to learn to perform the spin.

Draw upon my experience from this very recent example if ever you have any fears that prevent you from accomplishing something. Having gone through it recently, I can tell you that fear is fake. It is an illusion. Never let it stop you from living your life.

If you have any phobias, I urge you to overcome them. Go to an expert to really take it head-on if it is something daunting for you. There is one person I worked with in the past who had a phobia of chewing gum. This person would literally freeze when seeing someone chewing gum. The fear was real to that individual. Any fears you have in life, you must break them for your own freedom. Ask for help if need be. It is a sign of strength if it is for your betterment.

Utilise these winning habits and live your life the way you are meant to—a life of freedom. As for recognising the universal energy, you will only begin to see this the more you take notice of your surroundings. Coincidences will begin to occur, and then you'll realise there are no coincidences. When you are thinking of a song and it plays somewhere randomly, that is when it will happen. You could be walking through a shopping centre and you hear the song you were thinking about. A cup of coffee that you wanted at that very moment could be given to you by a friend or client, and you never asked for it.

The more coincidences you begin to notice, the more you will realise the intention you have towards each day dictates the events that occur. I have seen the contrast of receiving coincidences and being really grateful every time no matter how small. It almost appears miraculous when speaking about it to other people, even though they have no belief in it when you tell your story.

There is one moment that comes to mind at a workplace I was at, where I was looking for a box of plastic dividers for organisation in the warehouse. For two weeks, no one had seen the box I was looking for. One day, I was intent on finally finding out where it was. As I walked into a back room. I stood there looking forward, and all of a sudden a box fell from the shelf. That box had been up there for many weeks.

As I walked over to the box, inside it was what I was looking for. Not magic, not ghosts—it was just pure trust and faith of receiving what I wanted for a good cause and positive intent. A bulletproof mind is the foundation which leads to allowing yourself to feel deserving of all great things that come to you.

CHAPTER 15

Conclusion: Aligning the Choices We Make with Our Ultimate Desire

The information in the preceding chapters, I have full trust in, as I live by this. It has not been something I've implemented overnight. This is the result of analysing my life from my own journey and crafting my own destiny by living the past fifteen years with a mission to be the best version of myself. It has been fifteen years of a cocktail of emotions and intense situations that happened.

The action of all this is the real part that makes our life into a gem. How are you (and I) going to consistently implement this into our lives—to bite our bullets and be free to move forward? The journey never stops, but we must enjoy the journey of life without having those regrets towards the end.

I genuinely want everyone to feel the inner peace and power to tackle life head-on, no matter what situation may arise. Once you find and have this inner peace of mind, you will be able to glide through the rest of life. An automated confidence within you will transfer to every aspect of your life: personal, work, relationships, you name it.

Remember the formula:

- Give yourself a purpose. Set goals for yourself.
- Become confident with the leap of faith and spitting out the past pain.

- Analyse your relationships. Do they help you progress or hinder you?
- Create an action plan where you respect yourself by respecting time and filling it with quality development. This is an integral part of the journey where you begin to take solid action by sticking to the plan that you have created and adhering to the days set.

Aligning with our ultimate desire means we are living authentically. When you are sitting in your rocking chair, old and grey, what is it you want to be replaying in your mind at that moment? Is it that you accomplished everything you wanted to do, or is it that you are holding on to regrets that held you back?

If we learn from a lot of elderly people how they felt in old age, it is almost certain they all miss their youthful selves, where they were able to participate in many activities. None of us can imagine getting old whilst we are young right now or feel young. The physical element mentioned throughout allows us to keep that fire within. The elderly person mentioned before, Fauja Singh, is the perfect example of how our health and well-being are in our own hands. He went through a lot of trauma, but it was his will to live we should all gain inspiration from.

The *Bite Your Bullet* journey is one of strong self-belief and projecting confidence that you are invincible in an authentic manner. When you do this, you are indeed the controller of your destiny. The techniques outlined thus far are there to clear your past baggage. Don't be afraid to ask for assistance on tasks where you want to self-develop. Biting your bullet is something we need to encourage to create power within all people. Unleashing the power begins with unleashing our own ultimate desire.

It is time to implement these learnings into your life and never stray from the progress. Consistency and reviewing, plus repetition of your action steps, is how you will remain bulletproof. Develop trust and faith in the universal power. It transcends all cultures and beliefs, as it has no bias towards anyone or anything. This is the power of the universe, and we are all expressions of the universe living in a human form.

The winning mentality is the truth we all are. This includes the rest of nature. The plant that grows, the spider that catches the fly in its web, the apple tree that produces an apple, the lion that catches its prey, the sun's energy that gives life to Earth—and then there is us, humans. What is our nature? To reproduce like animals? To have lots of money? To own a car? Farm food? The nature of a human is the most complex, as we have the power to decide what our win is.

The animals, plants, and even the sun are winning by being true to their nature. Decide what nature you have about yourself and make that your win. That is why the choices you make should always match your ultimate desire. The plant that grows does not decide that it wants to fly like a bird. A spider will not decide to build a web in order to have a luxurious web. The apple tree will not suddenly decide to produce oranges. A lion will not decide to go and eat vegetation when it desires meat to survive. The wins for these elements of nature are being themselves.

When looking at it from this perspective, the human power of choice we have gives us many ultimate desires, which also produce the stress involved with this unlimited amount of choice. This is the beauty you can choose to focus in on when you determine what your ultimate desire may be. I hope you feel a sense of determination and focus for knowing what choices to make to reach your ultimate desire and prioritising yourself to win.

The icing on the cake of our lives is the ability to transcend man-made fears—or in this case, bullets. Go live your life. Be life. Bite your bullet! Call the shots!

Printed in Great Britain
by Amazon